HAVELLS

HAVELLS

THE UNTOLD STORY OF

QIMAT RAI GUPTA

ANIL RAI GUPTA

PORTFOLIO
PENGUIN

PORTFOLIO
Published by the Penguin Group
Penguin Books India Pvt. Ltd, 7th Floor, Infinity Tower C, DLF Cyber City,
Gurgaon 122 002, Haryana, India
Penguin Group (USA) Inc., 375 Hudson Street, New York, New York 10014, USA
Penguin Group (Canada), 90 Eglinton Avenue East, Suite 700, Toronto,
Ontario, M4P 2Y3, Canada
Penguin Books Ltd, 80 Strand, London WC2R 0RL, England
Penguin Ireland, 25 St Stephen's Green, Dublin 2, Ireland (a division of
Penguin Books Ltd)
Penguin Group (Australia), 707 Collins Street, Melbourne, Victoria 3008, Australia
Penguin Group (NZ), 67 Apollo Drive, Rosedale, Auckland 0632, New Zealand
Penguin Books (South Africa) (Pty) Ltd, Block D, Rosebank Office Park,
181 Jan Smuts Avenue, Parktown North, Johannesburg 2193, South Africa

Penguin Books Ltd, Registered Offices: 80 Strand, London WC2R 0RL, England

First published in Portfolio by Penguin Books India 2016

Copyright © Anil Rai Gupta 2016

ISBN 9780670088812

Typeset in Sabon by Manipal Digital Systems, Manipal
Printed at Replika Press Pvt. Ltd, India

A PENGUIN RANDOM HOUSE COMPANY

*To my mother, Vinod Gupta, who was the real force
behind QRG's success and who emotionally moulded me*

'*If my mind can conceive it, and my heart can believe it—then I can achieve it.*'

Muhammad Ali

CONTENTS

ACKNOWLEDGEMENTS

I am a firm believer that all men are born equal but only a handful rise above the ordinary. They are made of the same flesh and bone as others, yet somehow they manage to achieve superhuman feats. That is how a life becomes a story—a book.

My father, Qimat Rai Gupta, was one such man. He rose above his humble origins and overcame several physical ailments to build a business that is spread across the globe and, more importantly, has earned the respect of its peers.

His accomplishments were great, yet few outside his close-knit circle know about him.

The idea of this book came to me in 2010 after we had managed to bring Sylvania back from the brink of disaster. As I pondered over the sequence of events and marvelled at QRG's stellar leadership, it dawned on me that people would benefit greatly from reading about his life.

Of course, most sons think of their father as the ultimate hero, and I am no different. Yet, even when I thought objectively, it was clear to me that this was one story that had to be told.

I discussed this idea with QRG. He was reluctant—I ought to have known. He had always kept a low profile. What mattered to him was the brand equity of Havells and not personal glory. The book, he thought, would amount to self-promotion, something he had avoided all his life.

I had to work hard to convince him. QRG was headstrong but also a consensus builder. If his core team said something, he would give it serious thought. When the senior Havells team told him in one voice that the book was a good idea and not necessarily a publicity gimmick, he agreed to recount his life journey.

The project started in 2013 but was hampered by QRG's frequent ailments.

He passed away in November 2014. After that, this book became some kind of a mission for me. My family, friends and colleagues at Havells encouraged me to finish it as quickly as possible. It took a lot of effort and was, at times, emotionally draining but I stayed the course because I believed in QRG's and Havells's story.

I have been truthful in the book. It couldn't have been otherwise. That's the way I was brought up by my parents. There were constant discussions at home about family, business, and above all, values. I can say without hesitation that honesty is in my DNA. I can't be grateful enough to my parents for this.

What also helped was that there were frequent retellings of the past at home. My parents loved to recount anecdotes and events, which in hindsight turned out to be a treasure trove of information for this book. My parents kept an open house and therefore visitors were frequent—the tales they recounted also proved invaluable when I sat down to record the life and times of QRG.

Alam Srinivas spent a lot of time with QRG, the extended family, dealers and Havells employees. He helped gather the basic building blocks for this book. Without his Herculean effort, this book would not have been possible.

Pranjal Sharma helped QRG open up about things that happened in the past, some of which were new even to me. A good journalist is one who can make the other person disclose his innermost thoughts and experiences. That has made the text richer. Bhupesh Bhandari's suggestions were useful.

Vicky Gupta and Rajiv Goel from Havells and my sister, Geeta Agarwal, helped with facts, figures and information right from the beginning. Their observations were insightful and their interventions were critical. My friends, Puneet Bhatia, Ashish Bharatram and Tejpreet Chopra, whose fine sense of judgement I trust fully, gave valuable advice on the manuscript. If you are an 'insider', some obvious things escape your attention at times, and that is where well-meaning friends help. I am grateful to each one of them. Big thanks to Lohit Jagwani of Penguin Random House—for his infectious enthusiasm and sound advice.

My wife, Sangeeta, and friend Itiva Chopra, helped a lot to improve the language and presentation. I shall always be grateful to them for their help in giving shape to my thoughts.

ONE

Introduction: Business with Conviction and Empathy

Sometime in November 2014, I moved into the corner office at QRG Towers—a large office complex located near the expressway that runs from Noida to Greater Noida. The office was big and could comfortably accommodate over ten people. Until recently, the occupant of this room was my father, Qimat Rai Gupta, chairman and managing director of Havells and chairman of Sylvania. He was Bhaisahib to older employees and QRG to the rest of the world.

He had recently passed away after a brief illness. It was now my job to helm the business he had built from scratch. We had operations across continents and products across various categories, including electrical goods—consumer durables, switchgear, cable and wires, and lighting and fixtures. Then there were business associates, employees, vendors, dealers, bankers and investors to manage.

As I sat on the swivel chair behind the heavy wooden desk and looked over the busy highway to Greater Noida, memories of QRG's extraordinary life and sterling character flashed through my mind. I had very big shoes to fill.

He was not trained as an engineer but was a master in human engineering. He had no MBA degree but he knew what it took for a business to succeed. He may not have been a numerical wizard but he was one of the best wealth creators I have known. He may not have understood the whims and fancies of the stock market but he sure knew how to take care of shareholders.

Born into a household of modest means, QRG left his family with a net worth of $2 billion. Yet, he always remained humble and grounded. He could have afforded all the luxuries money can buy but chose to live simply. Our house was comfortable, never ostentatious. His cars were never extravagant. It was almost as if he knew that fortune can be fickle. That is why he chose to stay away from the limelight, and always focused on the job at hand.

QRG was not highly educated but his sharp and incisive intellect was second to no one's. He was not beholden to any guru and seldom found time for management books, yet he understood the value of brands, carried out several financial innovations and made stellar strategic acquisitions. He never took notes at meetings but could rattle off all the details without missing a single fact. Business, he often used to say, is done with conviction and not with a calculator.

He conducted business the old-fashioned way—with trust and empowerment. He detested corruption and unfair trade practices. He was flexible in his approach and was always open to new ideas. He had a childlike enthusiasm for innovation. Not once did he let his ego get the better of his business instincts.

Perhaps QRG's greatest skill was in man-management. There was some innate wisdom that gave him great insights into human behaviour. He was fond of films and soaps, and the morning after watching them, he would relate those stories to management practices.

His enthusiasm and confidence were contagious. Once, Naresh Gupta, his younger sister Sarla's husband, came with an acquaintance who wanted to start a business. QRG promised to help, only if Nareshji would also take the plunge. The meeting had a profound effect on Nareshji— both he and his friend quit their jobs and became business partners in no time!

To the world outside, he embodied every quality Dale Carnegie recommended in his path-breaking 1936 book, *How to Win Friends and Influence People*. He was lavish in his praise and slow to blame. Even if he did not like a person—and his instincts were mostly correct—he wouldn't be rude to him. 'What do I gain by being blunt with him?' he would ask. 'Criticism is futile.'

His empathy for the weak was evident. On his fiftieth wedding anniversary, he got fifty poor couples married— without any pomp or show. Human values were important for him. QRG would often tell our engineers to be 'good human engineers'.

Once, when he was a trader in old Delhi's cramped Bhagirath Palace, QRG had sent a worker to another trader on an errand. I don't know what got into the other trader's head and he slapped the worker. QRG marched up to him and told him sternly that in insulting his employee, he had insulted him, which was unacceptable.

On another occasion, Baba Ramdev had come to our home. His popularity was at its peak those days, so all our acquaintances and the entire neighbourhood had come for his darshan. QRG saw a chauffeur craning his neck from the verandah to get a glimpse of the high-profile visitor. He asked him to come forward and have his moment with Baba Ramdev.

There were times when QRG let somebody in need use his car while he was happy to travel in an autorickshaw himself. All visitors to our household would be received and seen off by him, whatever unearthly hour they chose to come and go. Small courtesies, like asking people if they had partaken of a meal, never escaped him.

At work, he took on a different persona. He would never hesitate to speak the truth, even if it made someone uncomfortable. And he would do so in public. For those who were new to the organization, this would come as a culture shock. Many would come and complain to me. 'He does the same to me,' I would tell them in all truthfulness.

What else would you expect from a man who would talk to his wife on the speakerphone in the presence of half a dozen people? He was that open and transparent. He expected the same from others.

Once people realized that he spoke plainly not to make them uncomfortable but to get the work done and to help them improve themselves, they accepted him as he was. That is why the attrition among employees who spend more than a year in Havells has always been low and the senior team is extremely stable.

In spite of his perceived bluntness, QRG was a great motivator. He could get ordinary people to deliver extraordinary results. His motto was: if a six-foot-tall man comes to you, make sure he feels seven feet tall when he leaves. He believed that people needed to be made aware of their latent strengths.

People would come out of meetings with him fully charged. He would stretch their imagination and motivate them to give more than they felt they were capable of—much like when Ram got Hanuman to deliver extraordinary results in the Ramayana. He would empower them to take decisions, though he would discuss the progress of the work with them frequently.

He would often address people as *dost*, or friend, when he wanted to encourage them to do something. That simple word used to have a magical impact on them. A lot of people would say that QRG had the habit of creating more QRGs! And whenever there was a crisis, and there were quite a few in his lifetime, some new fountain of energy and conviction would spring inside him.

In most large corporations, people work in boxes, and their work is reviewed once in a quarter. QRG broke all such silos. He would communicate with people all the time, yet encourage them to take decisions. 'If you want a man to go to Connaught Place,' he would say, 'don't tell him the way. Let him find it out for himself.' The employees felt like entrepreneurs themselves. 'If I take all the decisions, what are the employees there for?' he would argue.

That is why Havells, in spite of employing a large number of people, was never bureaucratic and lethargic—it was energetic and nimble like a small enterprise. The importance of quick decisions in the current times cannot be overemphasized.

QRG was a firm believer in open communication. His advice to people in trouble was: '*Kothe par chadkar bolo.*

Koi to sunega.' The message was: Only if you talk openly about your problems will a solution emerge. That led to the open culture at Havells. Newcomers and visitors often found it strange, and at times also a little disconcerting, but this is how he worked, and it served us well.

Havells is unique in another way—family and professionals coexist peacefully. QRG built it that way. In the initial years, he relied on Surjitji, my maternal uncle, to look after the technical aspects of the company. But as its scale of operations expanded, it was evident to him that the family would not be able to run it indefinitely. Professionals were brought in to replace family members in key positions.

The only two family members QRG retained were my cousin Ameet and me. But we were not given specific responsibilities—that task was left to the executives; instead, we were attached to his office. And there wasn't a single instance of special treatment being meted out to the family. 'Make the directors [family members] useless,' he would frequently exhort employees.

Of course, he wouldn't hesitate for a second before chastising Ameet and me if he felt we hadn't done the right thing. At times, it hurt, and sometimes I complained about it. But I would realize he had not done so out of any malice. Transparency was important for him. He would, in fact, often take it to unheard-of levels.

It also sent a very strong message to the employees that non-performance will not be tolerated in the organization, not even from family members.

We did have our differences, which is only natural, but there were never fissures between us. This was important.

Many business families have gone through what is called the Aurangzeb Syndrome—father and son fighting over the control of the business. This happens when the world views of father and son are different, resulting in a clash. This is what happened at Ranbaxy. According to *The Ranbaxy Story*, in the early nineties, Dr Parvinder Singh wanted to induct professionals into key positions and felt that the company needed to venture overseas in order to grow rapidly. Bhai Mohan Singh, his father, was uncomfortable with it. The two fought a nasty boardroom battle, in full view of the public, which resulted in Bhai Mohan Singh's bitter exit from Ranbaxy.

Such fights can destroy a company. Worse, there are people within every organization who feast on conflict. These fights take up all the time and, in the bargain, the company loses.

QRG and I knew that we had to avoid that at all costs. In our case, it helped that age did not restrain QRG's spirit—whatever I thought, he would think bigger. He would stretch any target I set. If I planned for Rs 100 crore, he would urge me to change it to Rs 300 crore.

I, too, made it a point not to complain about his decisions behind his back. Whenever somebody tried to instigate me against his decisions, I would say without hesitation, 'It must be fine if he has taken the decision.' My first reaction would be to defend his decision. That put a stop to all machinations. The hangers-on got the message. I extinguished my ego altogether.

Of course, QRG had an open mind and wouldn't mind reversing a decision after hearing others out. But we stood as one. While he was alive, QRG was the sole power centre in the company. I saw to it that no other message was ever conveyed to the employees through my actions. Of course, when he was bedridden at home because of illness, or was in hospital, I took the decisions; at all other times, he was the boss.

At home, QRG was the typical Indian father, strict and stern, especially when we were young. He never demonstrated his deep love for his children—that was left to our mother. But as we grew older, his affection became more visible. When any of us fell sick, he looked weak and vulnerable. And once my daughter and son were born, he dropped his guard further.

Dinner table discussions were seldom about business. He talked about values, which left a deep impression on us.

There were no restrictions imposed on us. QRG knew that imposing strict controls would be counterproductive. Still, we didn't do a lot of things that others of our age were doing because it just wasn't in our DNA. The family values we had imbibed kept us away from vices. We spent wisely and were never extravagant.

Family matters are complicated, especially when serious money is involved. India's corporate history is full of tales of family feuds. The only instance of an amicable separation is the Shriram family that split its business into three parts in 1989. In most other cases, there is acrimony.

QRG presided over three family splits—all were amicably done over glasses of lassi. He was practical and magnanimous in these divisions. That's why they generated zero bad blood. He had an open and friendly face, which made even complete strangers confide their deepest secrets in him.

Yet, his resolve was steely.

Throughout his adult life, QRG battled one ailment or the other—rheumatoid arthritis, dry eye syndrome, interstitial lung disease, kidney impairment, fractured spine and many more. But none of it managed to bog him down. Any other person would have succumbed to the negativity that diseases can generate. QRG proved more than equal to this challenge. In fact, his most fruitful years in business were the ones when he was battling these ailments.

He learnt to live with them. In 2005, he had to travel to Bangkok with some dealers for a promotional event. At the airport, he dislocated his right shoulder. He went to the doctor, got it fixed, and took the next flight to Bangkok!

After that incident, my mother learnt how to fix his shoulder whenever there was a dislocation. A few years later, we were in the midst of a dealer conference at Frankfurt when QRG dislocated his shoulder. My mother asked us to form a human curtain around him and quickly put the joint back into its socket. He went on to address the 400 delegates as if nothing had happened.

It was this resolve in him which helped us avert our biggest crisis—never mind that he was in his seventies by then! By the end of 2008, the global acquisition of Sylvania, which was hailed as brilliant and strategic by one and all the previous year, had started to look like a blunder and had brought us to the brink of collapse. The €220-million deal had stretched us financially. If it didn't work, we knew it could signal the beginning of the end for Havells. The global financial crisis had taken a severe toll on the business.

In the quarter that ended in September 2008, Sylvania incurred huge losses; more excruciatingly, the company breached its loan covenants. For the foreign bankers this simply meant our inability to repay the loans we had taken to aid the takeover. The global bankers put pressure on us to sell Sylvania to private equity players since we couldn't manage it.

However, we were determined not to let go of Sylvania. But that had started to look like empty bravado. The only way out was to pump more money into the company. We were told, by our highly paid advisers, to invest $3–5 million every month, for a year or so. Advice, in such circumstances, comes thick and fast. As QRG would say, *'Garib ki zoru, sabki sali'* (nobody respects a weak man).

For us, it was too much of a financial risk. To invest another $36–60 million in one year would have leveraged us beyond our limits. If the gamble failed, the stress would have finished Havells as well. All seemed lost.

One day in December 2008, QRG summoned Ameet and me to his office. Sylvania's performance, he told the two of us in no uncertain terms, was a blow to Havells's reputation. If we could not turn it around, he said, we would never again be able to do any acquisition. No banker would ever support us again. We had, QRG reminded us, not managed Sylvania hands-on, and had been happy to play the role of a financial investor. *'Shikaar jab tak khud nahin maaro, woh marta nahin hai,'* he said in his homespun wisdom—to really get the job done, you have to do it yourself.

This candid talk did the trick. In very simple words, he had laid bare the problem of Sylvania and also its solution.

Over the next year or so, we set about fixing the problems in earnest. Unviable factories and offices were shut down, several functions were consolidated and people we thought were hampering the turnaround were eased out. By April 2009, it had started to become clear that Sylvania could be salvaged. After that, recovery was swift. By June 2010, a complete turnaround had been achieved.

I have often wondered what would have happened if QRG had not prodded us to salvage Sylvania. Merchant bankers would have lined up some buyers. We would have cut our losses. That is what many Indian businessmen have done. Backed by easy money and the buzz around frugal Indian management, several companies had acquired assets abroad. After the initial euphoria died down, they didn't know what to do with these acquisitions.

But QRG was thinking long term. For him, the acquisition of Sylvania was not just an ego massage—he was convinced it fitted strategically into our vision of becoming a global player in the lighting business. Adverse financial performance, which could be fixed, did not change the fundamental premise of the takeover. He knew Sylvania's turnaround was a challenge, but he also saw in it an opportunity to prove our mettle.

Had it not been for him, the Sylvania story would have taken a totally different turn. Our reputation would have been in tatters. It was because of QRG that we came out of the crisis stronger and wiser.

While being headstrong helped in the case of Sylvania, QRG also had the capacity to know when strategic withdrawal made sense. In 1996, we had floated a joint venture with DZG of Germany to make electric meters. The business boomed between 1998 and 2002 when the World Bank gave huge loans to the electricity boards of various Indian states to shift from electromechanical to electronic meters.

But the World Bank's intervention also changed the contours of the business. Earlier, there were half a dozen organized players, and each one got a decent share of the state electricity boards' purchases. The World Bank's insistence on contracts to be offered through tenders to L-1 (lowest-priced) bidders opened the field for newcomers. Fly-by-night manufacturers mushroomed; some were even making meters in garages!

Prices crashed. At the same time, corruption increased. We were not sure whether it was worth our while to stake big bucks on an uncertain business. QRG decided to exit the meters business. In the beginning of 2002, we scaled it down; from Rs 60 crore in 1998, the annual revenues from the division had shot up to Rs 100 crore in 2000, and to Rs 300 crore in 2002. By 2005, it was worth Rs 100 crore a year, back to the 2000 level. In the next four to five years, we completely shut down the meters division.

His logic was simple, yet elegant. As a business house, we had limited managerial bandwidth. Were we ready to squander it on low-margin government orders, which were open to manipulation, or were we going to use it in a market that offered better profit margins and had less scope for corruption? What were the kind of competencies we wanted to build in our organization?

A large number of business houses are happy to operate in sectors that are heavily controlled—and hence open to 'gentle persuasion'. But QRG felt that wouldn't help a company survive in the long run.

Long before it became fashionable to talk about ethical business practices, QRG, with his innate wisdom, knew the right way.

A company that chases business through unfair means almost always ends up breeding corruption within itself. It eats up the organization from the inside. Executives think only of enriching themselves, instead of working for the company's future. It is through such choices that a leader sets the direction for the rest of the organization. It takes courage and conviction to wind down a business that fetches you Rs 300 crore—half of the company's annual turnover.

Havells was always the focus of his attention. In the 1990s, prompted by easy liquidity, many business houses diversified into new areas, which often had nothing to do with their mainline business. It was only after a few years that the whole concept of core competence came up. By then, a lot of companies had burnt cash in unproductive ventures. Some were even driven to the brink of bankruptcy.

There was much discussion within our family too. Opportunities were mushrooming all over the place; if we delayed, we might miss the bus and lose the first mover advantage, many people told us. After much deliberation, we set up two new businesses: Havells Financial Services and Zeus Advertising. Within a year, it dawned on us that these businesses required more attention than we were in a position to provide. We brought down the shutters on both the businesses right away.

After that, whenever a new business proposal came to us, we would ask, 'How much effort and focus will it require?' Real estate was one option we considered seriously in 2006–07. The market was booming. Prices had shot through the roof. We said, 'Why don't we set up Havells apartments, with our own switches, fans, wires and lights?' Thankfully, the idea never even reached the drawing board.

A few years after that, it was suggested to us that we should get into power generation—as some kind of backward integration! We were tempted. I spoke to a couple of friends who had invested in the sector. Their advice confirmed our worst fears—because of high government intervention we decided to exit the meters business. We had no appetite for a sector that required us to cut clandestine deals. So we said 'no' to power as well.

As a result of this focus, Havells continued to grow. It got our uninterrupted attention. It is not easy to resist temptation, especially when all others around you are succumbing to it.

The only diversification we actively pursued was healthcare. A friend had approached me with an offer to buy a hospital in Faridabad. That is how QRG Hospital and Research Centre came up. After that, we set up QRG Health City, also in Faridabad.

The investment was made by the family, not Havells. Therefore, it did not impact Havells's shareholders at all. Charity is the preserve of businessmen, not companies.

Any company's task is to maximize shareholders' wealth, not undertake charity. This may sound impersonal but it is the truth. In the West, Bill Gates does charity out of his personal wealth, not through the cash reserves of Microsoft.

That's why many commentators have rightly found fault with the mandatory 2 per cent (of net profit) that companies are required to spend on corporate social responsibility.

The time-tested model in healthcare is to draw in as many patients as possible, and then extract as much money from them as possible. Doctors are encouraged to write tests and processes that are wholly unnecessary. With the government's healthcare delivery system in a shambles, people have no option but to come to private hospitals. Private hospitals make profits by maximizing patient cost. This starts the moment patients walk into the hospital.

We used to discuss it often but did not know how to fix the problem.

In 2014, I was diagnosed with autoimmune pancreatitis, a rare disorder. There was some concern that it could also be cancer. Doctors advised me to go abroad and get it checked. I didn't want to take chances and went to the famous Mayo Clinic in Minnesota for diagnosis.

There, thankfully, they confirmed it wasn't cancer. But while I was there, I carefully studied its practices. The hospital, which has more than 3300 physicians, scientists and researchers on its rolls, did not give a percentage of the profit to doctors for bringing in patients or prescribing tests. I thought it would be nice to have a similar system in place in our hospitals.

When I discussed it with QRG, he jumped with joy. It was a good idea and he was ready to support it. We immediately changed the entire remuneration system of our doctors.

We agreed to hire doctors for our hospitals on fixed salaries. They would not have any financial targets—they were only entitled to regular increments. Thus, when we hired doctors, we just looked at their clinical expertise, and there was no discussion of financial performance.

And we did not offer premium salaries. We told our doctors that they needed to work fixed hours, and didn't have to kill themselves to achieve any kind of financial targets. At the end of the day, they could look forward to spending time at home with their families. The idea appealed to many doctors.

This is yet another example of how QRG had an open mind and was willing to go against conventional wisdom. Age could not curb his entrepreneurial energy and enthusiasm. If a man gets excited about a new idea even in his advanced age, surely there is nothing more he can ask from God.

In a sense, QRG was conservative as well as unconventional. In ethics, he was old-fashioned and unadventurous. He would never do anything that was improper. But when it came to work, he was innovative and open. He had the ability to look beyond the obvious. He had bought Havells in 1971—just the brand. At that time, such an acquisition was unheard of.

Business, thanks to the Licence Raj, was completely geared towards production. Havells, a new company that he set up, purchased products from a local factory and sold them under its brand. In 1976, the annual turnover from trading was Rs 3–4 crore. Given his modest beginnings in life, QRG ought to have been satisfied with the state of affairs—the money was good enough to take care of him and his family. Yet, his mind was ticking away.

By that time, QRG was convinced that trading had limited scope. He could grow up to a point, but not beyond it unless he had a brand and a factory of his own. The obvious benefit was that he would be able to control the quality of the products he sold. Also, the profit margins in trading are always low; if you want to improve the margins, you need to have your own factories—that is where the maximum value is added.

Therefore, in 1976, after outsourcing products for five years under the Havells brand, he set up a small assembly unit that made switchgear for use in homes and factories. This was set up in a rented basement premises in west Delhi's Kirti Nagar.

There was no looking back after that. Over the next few years, more factories sprang up in and around Delhi. In 1979, a second factory to make High Rupturing Capacity fuse (HRC fuse) which is used to save electric equipment from high voltage, was set up at Badli, Delhi; a third factory the next year was started in west Delhi's Tilak Nagar to make electric meters, both for industrial and residential use.

In 1983, QRG took a bank loan to fund the Rs 35 lakh purchase of Towers and Transformers, a sick company whose promoters he knew, primarily because of the company's ten-acre plot in Sahibabad, an area adjoining east Delhi. Later, he set up a new plant for electric meters there.

In the years that followed, many more manufacturing units were acquired. Many of them are the best in the country in their categories—the gold standard. Some are even comparable to the best in the world.

When it came to quality, QRG would tolerate no compromises. The products we made had to be the best; the various agencies we worked with had to excel. It was an obsession for him. Even if it meant significantly higher expenditure, so be it. QRG did not believe in cutting corners.

Today, if Havells is able to sell across the world, it is because of its strong manufacturing base. Our products are second to none in quality and our prices are competitive. The foundation for this excellence in manufacturing was laid by QRG almost four decades ago.

Similarly, QRG was the first to realize that electrical products would evolve from a commodity-like market to one in which brands would become all important. In 2007, Havells was the leader in domestic switchgear, second in cables after Finolex, second in switches after Anchor, fourth in fans, and second in lighting after Philips. These were product categories with strong brands (Philips and Osram in lighting, Crompton Greaves, Orient, Polar and Khaitan in fans, Finolex in cables, for example) but companies spent an insignificant part of their turnover on brand promotion. And a large part of that was below the line. In categories like switchgear and cable, such expenditure was zero.

This is when QRG said that if Havells had to stand out in the market, it had to break the clutter by radically outspending its rivals. From around Rs 15 crore, the budget for brand building was ramped up to Rs 80 crore. At that time, it was over 4 per cent of Havells's turnover. He wanted to communicate directly with our consumers.

We signed on Lowe Lintas to devise a campaign. R. Balakrishnan, popularly known as Balki, now the chairman and chief creative officer, got involved. The brand, it was decided, would talk to men between twenty-five and forty-five years of age (electrical fittings are selected by men, tiles and bathroom fittings by women), and for that, cricket would be the right medium.

Fortunately for us, that was the time India had fared poorly in the World Cup in the West Indies. Cricket properties were going dirt cheap, and Havells was able to strike some amazing advertising deals. It proved to be a game changer.

Ever since, QRG kept the bar for advertisements high. Some didn't work, like the one for Havells fans that showed people wading through a pool of sweat, but mostly they were high quality.

This gave us all the advantages that strong brand equity can fetch.

One immediate benefit was that the discount at which Havells sold its lamps and fixtures in the market soon vanished. Over the years, Havells became the most recognized brand in all its categories. Its recall value became almost universal.

A powerful brand is a good way for a manufacturer to move up the value chain. And that is the space QRG always wanted to operate in. Thus, when we entered the fan market, QRG decided to offer world-class products, even if it meant that consumers had to pay premium prices.

This was going against the grain of the market. For the half a dozen large players, and a slew of smaller players, who competed in the unorganized segment that comprised half the overall fan market, pricing was of the essence. To tackle competition from the smaller players, who sold at cheap prices (thanks to malpractices, including evasion of taxes), the large manufacturers resorted to outsourcing to cut costs. The basic rules of the game were to sell at rock-bottom prices, attain volumes, and operate at wafer-thin margins.

QRG refused to play by those rules. Everyone said our strategy of high-quality, high-price fans was wrong. At the launch conference in 2004, most of our 400-odd distributors and dealers predicted that we would fail unless we introduced low-priced fans. Our senior managers felt the same way. QRG refused to give in to their demand. He did not wish to be a follower. *'Sau sawar Dilli chale, toh aap bhi chal diye,'* he would often run down the herd mentality with discernible derision.

The strategy worked; today, we are one of the largest manufacturers of fans in the country. And in the premium category, we are the undisputed leader.

But his real forte was dealership management.

I often recall the story of Rakesh Mehrotra, who started as a small dealer of Havells in Kanpur in 1979, and is today an associate director of the company. No other story exemplifies QRG's close relationship with his dealers better.

Mehrotra first met QRG in April 1982. In 1981–82, he had done business worth Rs 1.37 lakh for Havells in Kanpur and promised to raise it to Rs 3 lakh in 1982–83. QRG raised the target to Rs 3.6 lakh. A little unnerved, Mehrotra asked QRG, 'What about my profits?'

QRG told him, 'You take care of Havells and we will take care of you.' In a flash, Mehrotra became beholden to him. That year, he did business of over Rs 6 lakh!

Over the years, QRG made him feel special on several occasions. A couple of years after the first meeting, Mehrotra mentioned to Surjitji, my uncle and QRG's brother-in-law, that his family wanted a Sony television. At that time, it cost Rs 20,000—significantly more expensive than the incentives companies like Havells gave to their dealers. The next day, after he had spoken to QRG, Surjitji asked Mehrotra to buy the television and send the bill to him!

In 1988, Mehrotra's sister was to get married. QRG called the accounts department and asked it not to put pressure on Mehrotra for payment. QRG attended the wedding, and was among the first to arrive and the last to leave.

A few years later, the family that Mehrotra's sister was married into ran into some financial problems. So much so that it decided to abandon Kanpur. Mehrotra, who was very close to his sister, was shaken by the crisis and had to resort to taking sedatives to sleep.

When QRG heard about this, he called Mehrotra. If he was expecting words of sympathy, Mehrotra was mistaken. After saying that he would always support him, QRG admonished Mehrotra for being despondent and taking recourse to sedatives. It had the desired effect. Mehrotra shed the negativity and sorted out the problem.

Years later, when Mehrotra's mother was terminally ill, QRG and my mother visited her in Kanpur and spent the entire day with her.

This personal touch had a transformative effect on Mehrotra—from a dealer, he went on to become a distributor, then the agent for the whole of Uttar Pradesh and finally an associate director! In fact, QRG felt a similar sense of concern for all his dealers. They were like family to him.

QRG had a practical approach towards technology—it was not an end in itself but a means to delight the consumer. In every line of our business, he identified the best technical people in the industry and tried to get them on board.

Till the 1990s, it was easy to shop for technology from boutique firms in the West. After that, QRG was quick to realize that pure technology companies in the West were gradually becoming part of multinational corporations, and this could curtail Havells's access to products. That is when he began to insist that we should invest more in technology. And that quest would play a vital role in our acquisition-led growth strategy in the future.

The idea of this book took shape after Sylvania's future was salvaged. It was during that period that I realized what I had possibly known instinctively—QRG's management style was unique. It was distinct from the manner in which most family-owned businesses are managed in India, and it was different from the way in which professional global conglomerates are run.

The second reason why I thought this book was important was because QRG never got the credit and recognition he deserved within the business community. In the domestic fast-moving electrical goods sector, QRG enjoyed a venerable status. In the global lighting arena, Sylvania is renowned. In some sections of the national society, where our group initiated large social work projects, he was respected and revered. However, when it comes to overall national or international recognition, he was, and remains, a relatively unknown figure.

His relative obscurity was not by design—it was forced on him because of his ill health. As a result, I became the public face of Havells. A lot of people held the view that I steered the course. This was at best a half-truth. I wanted to set the record straight. The rise of Havells would not have happened without QRG.

The third reason for writing this book is that QRG and I were a good example of how father and son could work together in business. I know of so many cases where this sort of understanding does not exist. Between QRG and I, we came up with a template that worked well. A lot of business families could draw lessons and use them in their own lives.

I felt a strong urge to document my father's life and accomplishments. I thought it would also help the thousands of our existing and future employees and managers across the globe to understand his management philosophy. It would benefit other global stakeholders—our distributors, dealers, shareholders, lenders and consumers.

More importantly, it could provide business and personal insights to millions of Indian and global managers, self-employed ambitious business persons, as well as budding executives who enter B-schools each year with entrepreneurial dreams.

QRG was a dreamer and a doer.

TWO

Get Me a Japanese Memsahib

Our roots are in Punjab, in a village not far from Malerkotla, a town of less than 1,00,000 people on the highway that connects Ludhiana with Sangrur. Before Independence, it was ruled by a Muslim Nawab, in what was predominantly a Sikh and Hindu territory.

Actually, the Nawab of Malerkotla was always well thought of by the Sikhs and Hindus. Legend has it that in 1705, when Wazir Khan, the governor of Sirhind, ordered the two sons of Guru Gobind Singh, the last of the Sikh Gurus, to be bricked alive, the Malerkotla Nawab, Sher Mohammad Khan, protested vehemently and asked for clemency. When none was shown, he stomped out of the court in protest. Guru Gobind Singh acknowledged this act of kindness. In the Sikh reprisal that followed, Malerkotla was therefore left alone.

Athra Mal, QRG's great-grandfather, lived in a village called Rajo Majra. Almost midway between Sangrur and Malerkotla is a small town called Dhuri. From here, one road leads to Barnala in the west. You will hit Rajo Majra soon after you start for Barnala on this road.

Athra Mal was a commission agent and had done fairly well for himself. Family lore has it that he was a frequent visitor to the royal court at Malerkotla and owned several properties in the town. Some of his kinsmen were known to keep elephants and camels as well, which was quite a status symbol in those days.

But the gains were frittered away by his only son, Sarwa Mal, not on vice but on charity. By all accounts, he was a large-hearted man who found it hard to say no to people who came to him for help. Sarwa Mal married a girl who was the sole survivor of a plague attack in her village. Clearly, he had a strong socialist bent of mind, something his later generations inherited in some measure.

Unfortunately, he did no work. So, the only way he could have sustained his charitable disposition was by selling the family silver. And that's precisely what happened. The family's fortunes began to dwindle.

Sarwa Mal had five sons: Lachhman Das (born in 1909), Lekh Raj (1913), Ganda Ram (1917), Om Prakash (1924) and Preetam Chand (1930). We are baniyas, who are well known in every corner of the country for their business acumen. The community derives its name from *vanijya*, Sanskrit for commerce. Yet, the sons of Sarwa Mal showed no special inclination towards business. Especially Lachhman Das, QRG's father, who took on odd jobs here and there, and later even started a business, was more inclined towards religion than anything else.

To be fair to them, business in north India was nascent in the pre-Independence days. There was only one company of any importance in the whole region—Delhi Cloth and General Mills Ltd, then run by Lala Shri Ram, which later became DCM Ltd. Business was capital intensive, and the financial markets here were underdeveloped. Trading was the only option available to people of the mercantile class. Sarwa Mal's sons showed no great skills.

The only exception was his fourth son, Om Prakash, or O.P. Gupta. There was a burning desire in him to do well so that the family could come out of the hard times it had fallen into. He was the first in the family to move out of Punjab in search of a job. His first job was in Coimbatore where he worked for a military contractor. His pay was Rs 40 per month. He ate at the canteen run by the contractor and sent the entire salary home to his father—such was his concern. Subsequently, he took up a job with a steel maker at Gobindgarh in Punjab.

In 1946, O.P. Gupta relocated to Calcutta, as Kolkata was known then. It so happened that his employer had sent him to Calcutta for some work. The prospects for growth in the city, which was once the imperial capital and was still a hub for industry, appealed to O.P. Gupta. He resigned from his job and moved to Calcutta bag and baggage.

That was the year of the infamous Calcutta riots. There was bad blood in the air. Bodies were strewn in the streets. But O.P. Gupta decided to take his chances. Initially, he lived in Central Avenue and rented a small office on Cotton Street. He first became an iron and steel merchant, buying and selling the commodity. But the going was tough. All trade was controlled by the Marwaris and they were not ready to trust an outsider. Still, by dint of sheer hard work, O.P. Gupta was eventually able to gain their confidence. Word got around in the city's trading circles that the Punjabi *chhokra* (lad) was trustworthy. In 1948, he got married and made Calcutta his home.

Soon after, O.P. Gupta started a trading company called O.P. Gupta & Brothers. He made his two brothers, Lachhman Das and Ganda Ram, partners in this company so that they could also make some money—such was his concern for his family. The two brothers lived in Calcutta with him for some time. But it was clear that O.P. Gupta was running the show. This was particularly hard for Ganda Ram Gupta who was the more ambitious of the two. The duo therefore decided to leave Calcutta and come back to Punjab. In 1958, O.P. Gupta left the iron and steel business and got into electrical products. He housed that business under a company he had set up in 1952 called O.P. Gupta and Co.

Lachhman Das was a simple and saintly man. He wasn't destined for greatness. He sired seven children, three boys and four girls—Kewal Krishna (born in 1930), Kanta (1934), QRG (1937), Kamla (1939), Kailash (1942), Sarla (1945) and Surinder (1948).

There is an interesting story about QRG's infancy. In those days, families used to sleep on the terrace during summer. The bedrolls would be carried up at night and, in the morning, after everybody was up and about, these would be thrown down on to the courtyard to be picked up later. One day, Lachhman Das rolled up one of the bedrolls and flung it down, unaware that his two-month-old son, QRG, wrapped up in the sheets, was still sleeping on it! Miraculously, the child escaped unhurt.

The elders in the family saw this as some sort of divine signal and called the family priest, pundit Jagannath, to draw up the boy's horoscope.

The pundit, after inquiring about the date and time of birth, drew his chart and concluded the boy would one day rise to great heights, so much so that he would be surrounded by cars. That, after all, was the time when only the super-rich could afford cars. But moving around in a car was such a distant dream for the family that everybody joked that QRG was destined to become a traffic controller at some road intersection!

QRG started his studies at the Sanatan Dharam School in Malerkotla. Those who knew him from that time would say he was a child prodigy who excelled in studies.

Most importantly, QRG had dreams in his heart. In those conservative times, children were brought up differently. They were not allowed to dream but had to toe the line their parents dictated. Perhaps parents were just being practical. Thanks to the limited opportunities available for betterment, dreams often ended in heartbreak. To prevent this outcome, dreams were nipped in the bud. It is a sad commentary on the times—there was little chance for most Indians to turn their dreams into reality.

O.P. Gupta, QRG's uncle, was the first to realize that the boy was thinking of life beyond small-town Punjab. Once, when O.P. Gupta was going back to Calcutta after a vacation, he asked everybody at home what he should bring for them on his next visit. When it was young QRG's turn, he asked for a Japanese memsahib! While others laughed it off, O.P. Gupta knew that the young lad's mind was ticking away, and that nothing could confine him to a small town in Punjab. He would recall this incident till his last days.

THREE

Baby Steps in Business

Even as a child, QRG observed keenly all that was happening around him. Thus, he noticed with grave concern the state of his family. His father, Lachhman Das, was not earning enough and was thus sinking deeper into debt with each passing month. Who would feed the large family? Who would pay for his sisters' weddings? It was considered a disgrace by society if families were not able to get their daughters married by a certain age. These questions worried young QRG tremendously. The issues that bothered O.P. Gupta now began to give QRG sleepless nights.

Lachhman Das's in-laws, who had a small business in Khanna—a district in Ludhiana—asked him to join them. Their company, Jharu Mal Vilayati Ram, had a rolling mill at Gobindgarh and also sold kerosene. They offered Lachhman Das a salary of Rs 200 per month.

This wouldn't have been an easy decision for my grandfather, one can imagine—it is deeply humiliating in that part of the country to take favours from the wife's family. But the situation was so dire that Lachhman Das had no option but to agree. In 1948, he swallowed his pride and relocated to Gobindgarh with his brood.

QRG's studies continued at Khanna, at his maternal grandfather's house. However, the family's precarious finances continued to bother him. The salary of Rs 200 his father earned was not enough and his father's debt had only increased. In 1953, after he had taken his matriculation exams, QRG knew education wasn't a luxury he could afford—he had to support his father. God willing, he would take up studies again in life, and that's how it actually played out (he attempted to complete his graduation while working, but this had to be aborted again due to his mother's ill health). He retained his love for reading and learning right till the end.

So, even before the exams were out, QRG became a drawing teacher in a local school on a monthly salary of Rs 90. After two months, he gave up that job and started to assist his father in the kerosene shop of Jharu Mal. It is not easy for a teenager to give up what he likes to do and get bogged down in mundane work. One can only imagine how much QRG was moved by his family's pitiable condition, and his empathy for his debt-ridden father.

Unknown to him, destiny had steered him towards what he was best at—business. Jharu Mal Vilayati Ram owned another small kerosene shop at a place called Chawa Pahal on the road to Ludhiana. It was losing money rapidly. QRG was asked to run that shop. It was more like an outpost. Customers didn't come to this shop, at least not in large numbers, and it was QRG's job to travel to nearby villages on his bicycle to sell kerosene. It was sold under the Suraj brand. *'Suraj marka mitti ka tel, raat ko din bana de'*, its tag line said, which meant that the Suraj brand of oil will turn dark nights into bright days.

QRG realized this was his opportunity. He turned around the loss-making shop at Chawa Pahal in no time. This was also the time he was able to put to practical use the wisdom his young but fertile mind had assimilated.

As a child, he had received two books from O.P. Gupta that had made a deep impact on his way of thinking. These were Dale Carnegie's *How to Win Friends and Influence People*, and Napoleon Hill's *Think and Grow Rich*.

When I told QRG about my plan to write this book, his first reaction was that I should write a book that was like Carnegie's. 'If people read it after 100 years, the book should still appeal to them and have knowledge that can help them improve their lives,' he said. The two books changed his life; till the end, he would tell everyone in the office and outside that they should read them.

From Carnegie, he learnt the art and science of building long-lasting personal networks and business relationships. He imbibed what the author, whose courses on relationships attract people almost six decades after his death, taught about the ways to handle people.

These included the ability to not criticize too much, give honest and sincere appreciation, become genuinely interested in others, be a good listener, make others feel important, show respect for others, admit one's mistakes, throw challenges, and many others. Later, those who knew him well would marvel at how QRG had no enemies. Some said he was like Bali of the Ramayana, the king of the monkey kingdom and elder brother of Sugriva, who could acquire half the strength of his enemies!

Hill's lessons were related to business leadership and entrepreneurship. Although QRG's pursuits were never materialistic and, therefore, he wasn't too excited about the 'grow rich' part of the book, he still realized that the author had insights for empire builders.

These included learnings such as 'the beginning of any achievement is a burning desire', 'the mind can achieve what it can conceive and believe', 'one is a master of one's own destiny', 'there are temporary defeats before success', 'every adversity or failure carries with it the seed of greater benefit', and 'it is imperative to maintain the highest standards of integrity'.

His first practical lessons in the art of building relationships were learnt as a teenager, when he visited the neighbouring villages of Chawa Pahal on a bicycle to sell kerosene to farmers. The people he met were rich feudal landlords, those who did not think twice before beating people up, or even murdering someone. One wrong word to them or their family members, and you were history.

'I knew from Carnegie and Hill that my first task was to know my customers well and be on a comfortable footing with them. I would address these landlords as *dadaji* (grandfather) and *veerji* (elder brother), and talk about personal issues with them. I wouldn't talk business but got to know them as elders. Although they did not buy anything from me then, they did so after a while,' QRG would recall.

Jack Carroll, world-renowned strategic sales management teacher and writer, maintained that the real art of salesmanship is the 'concealment of salesmanship—characterized by a quiet, relaxed, well-prepared salesperson who forgets every aspect of technique and just listens and reacts in real time'. This is exactly what QRG did with the landlords; he didn't sell them anything, he just spoke to them and made them feel that he was a part of their immediate social circle. The strategy worked well and they became his regular customers.

The dilemma QRG faced came from an unexpected quarter.

There was some pressure on QRG to adulterate kerosene for higher profits. This unethical practice made him distinctly uncomfortable. For advice, he turned to O.P. Gupta, who had by now become his friend, philosopher and guide. The two men had a similar style of thinking which had brought them closer. All through his life, QRG looked up to O.P. Gupta as his mentor. His uncle's advice was practical: 'First feed your stomach, and then think of such matters.'

It was practical advice but the idea of adulteration didn't appeal to QRG. By dint of sheer hard work, QRG had made a success of the Chawa Pahal shop. As a reward, it is possible that he got a share of the profit. With this money, he arranged for the weddings of his two sisters, Kanta and Kamla, in 1955, and also cleared all the debt that his father, Lachhman Das, had accumulated. He even managed to save a tidy sum of money for himself—Rs 9000.

Since O.P. Gupta worried all the time about his siblings, he called his youngest brother, Preetam Chand, or P.C. Gupta, who had completed his studies, over to Calcutta to work with him in his trading company, O.P. Gupta & Co.

In 1952 or so, P.C. Gupta got married. A few years later, he decided to relocate to Delhi. Having worked with his brother, he wanted to set up a similar enterprise in the capital. He took up a shop in Bhagirath Palace, the hub of the electrical equipment trade in Delhi, not far from Chandni Chowk.

The history of Chandni Chowk is fascinating. Built in 1650, the chowk, or the square, was an extension of the Red Fort (Lal Quila), Mughal Emperor Shah Jahan's palace on the banks of the Yamuna when he shifted his capital from Agra to Shahjahanabad (Delhi). The name of the market, designed by the emperor's daughter, Jahanara, is either because of its glimmer during moonlit nights or its silversmiths. *Chandni* could mean moonlight or a distortion of *chandi* (silver).

Bhagirath Palace's antecedents are more fascinating. It was the residence of Begum Samru (or Sumru), a nautch girl-turned-empress, who was the *bibi* of Walter Reinhardt, a German mercenary, who first fought with the French against the British in 1747, and later switched allegiance to the Mughals, as described by William Dalrymple in his book *The Last Mughal*.

Reinhardt's relationship with Samru, a Kashmiri whose original name was Farzana Zeb un-Nissa, began when she was fourteen or fifteen years, and her new name is an Indian version of sombre, which was Reinhardt's nickname because of his facial expression.

The Begum's penchant and skills in diplomatic intrigues were legendary and this was confirmed by her ability to negotiate with the East India Company, even though her proximity to the Mughals was known. Twice she helped the latter get out of trouble, and Emperor Shah Alam treated her like a daughter.

Akbar Shah, who succeeded Shah Alam, donated the garden in Chandni Chowk to the begum, where Bhagirath Palace was constructed. Now owned by the State Bank of India, it is in a dilapidated state despite being a heritage building. The begum's remaining inheritance is under various disputes.

Bhagirath Palace, a remnant of the Mughal dynasty, had become a wholesale market for electrical products sometime in the forties. P.C. Gupta set up his shop in this building, which measured about seventy square feet. Since he had come from Calcutta, where surnames like Mukherjee, Chatterjee and Banerjee were common, he named his shop Guptajee & Co. It started operations in January 1958.

The same year, in August, QRG came to Delhi on holiday and stayed with his uncle, P.C. Gupta, at his home in Daryaganj. In those days, it was considered impolite to stay in a hotel if you had relatives in a city.

Life was soon to change for QRG.

P.C. Gupta had to go out of town on a business trip, so he asked QRG to look after the shop for a few days. On his return, the uncle realized that sales had been brisk; he was impressed and, immediately, asked QRG to become his partner. P.C. Gupta, however, put forth a condition—since he had invested Rs 20,000 in the shop and its stock, QRG would have to pay him Rs 10,000 to become an equal partner.

QRG was stunned. He didn't know how to react. He implored P.C. Gupta to make his older brother, Kewal

Krishna, who was married and had kids at that time and was working in Chandigarh, his partner. But P.C. Gupta was adamant that he only wanted QRG as his business partner. After a while, QRG warmed up to the idea. He had saved Rs 9000, and he borrowed the remaining Rs 1000 from Raj Kumar, his younger sister Kamla's husband who lived in Pathankot near Jammu.

Before he knew it, QRG was in business in Delhi!

After a month or so, he decided to get his parents, two unmarried sisters, Kailash and Sarla, and his younger brother, Surinderji, over to Delhi. He had rented a small house in Krishna Nagar in the trans-Yamuna area, a new locality set up for people who had been displaced by Partition. The company that divided the plots and helped develop the mid-market colony was none other than DLF, one of India's largest and most valuable real estate developers today.

But convincing his parents to leave Gobindgarh was far from easy for QRG. My grandfather, Lachhman Das, opposed the move. He wanted QRG to start a grocery store in Gobindgarh instead. But QRG knew that the growth prospects in the small Punjabi town were limited. He would probably be comfortable as a grocer but if the family had to improve its station in life, he would have to build a future for himself in Delhi. Maybe in his mind, he had got a glimpse of the future!

A few years earlier, O.P. Gupta had told him about the possibilities that existed in larger cities. In a letter from Calcutta, he wrote to QRG: 'Here [currency] notes fly in the air. All you need is somebody to reach out and pluck them from the air.' The magic and wisdom of these words was not lost on QRG. His heart was set on moving to Delhi.

His parents were not too supportive of the idea of moving. They were probably apprehensive about starting from scratch in a new place. But QRG was persistent. At one stage, his mother even taunted him that since he now had money, he was trying to impose his will on others. QRG responded in the way that only he could. He gave his passbook to his mother and said, 'This [the move to Delhi] is not for my own benefit but for the whole family. Please keep the money I have saved if you think it has caused the discord.' Slowly, his folks saw his viewpoint and they all moved to Delhi.

'I persuaded my father. I convinced him that there was more potential in Delhi. The rest of the family stood by me. My father had no option, especially when his Calcutta-based brother said it was better to join me in Delhi with the rest of the family,' QRG would recall. O.P. Gupta's opinion was valued by all in the family.

FOUR

The Trader from Bhagirath Palace

By the time QRG settled down in his new business, there were about 100 shops at Bhagirath Palace, some as small as his, and others that were much bigger. The average turnover of individual shops was Rs 10,000 a month. For nine years (1958–67), Guptajee & Co. had similar earnings. Based on profit margins of 15–20 per cent and after deduction of costs, the two partners earned about Rs 500 to 1000 per family.

'Monthly expenses were the same, and the family spent whatever we earned. Business was consistent, but it did not grow much. My uncle was satisfied with this,' QRG would remember.

Strategies for the traders of Bhagirath Palace were fairly straightforward. The companies that manufactured electrical products had a quota system for the big wholesalers; the firms sold specific quantities based on the traders' past sales. The traders marked up the price by a certain margin, and pushed the products on to the retailers in the same and neighbouring cities and towns. Everyone made money, some less and others more.

The companies needed the distribution network. Guptajee & Co. dealt in cables, which were largely manufactured by two companies, Nicco Cable (which still exists, is headquartered in Kolkata and owned by Nicco Group whose chairman is Rajive Kaul) and Indian Cables. There was a clutch of smaller producers too.

Trading is the same these days as it was back then; there is a price difference between the wholesale and retail markets. So, a slightly smart middleman trader in the sixties, like Guptajee & Co., would buy cheap and sell with a slight mark-up.

Understanding the business was easy; it took QRG only a few days to figure out the products and their pricing structure, and seek profitable deals. 'My fellow traders were willing to teach me the tricks of the trade. How much time would it take for any intelligent person to learn these things? My advantage was that I had some experience in trading at the village level,' QRG would relate.

The transition and professional adjustment from a village to the capital city also wasn't difficult. 'I could converse fluently in Hindi. No one realized I was from Punjab; even later, very few people knew we were Punjabis,' QRG would say.

Guptajee & Co., in those early years, was not a fully fledged wholesaler; it did not have the contacts or financial clout to buy directly from the manufacturers. QRG and his uncle were not retailers, i.e. they did not sell to end-customers, institutional or individual.

They were essentially middlemen within the distribution chain; they procured from the wholesalers and sold to the retailers—either those who came to Bhagirath Palace to look for a bargain or those whom QRG approached during his travels to the smaller cities.

QRG, therefore, travelled to the bigger cities like Bombay, as Mumbai was called then, to purchase goods, and then to places like Kanpur and Meerut to sell them at a higher price.

Life was comfortable. Most traders would trudge in after 10.30 a.m., by which time QRG would have finished his routine work, including the accounts. After work, around the time the shops would shut, traders would congregate and gossip, share some chaat and chai. Competition was not cut-throat; people did not sacrifice personal relationships or human decency in the pursuit of wealth.

'We followed a routine. Get up at 6 a.m. and go for private coaching classes for a couple of hours in the morning before reaching the shop at 9 a.m. We packed up at 7 p.m. As I was doing my bachelor's in political science through correspondence, I studied after I reached home. Obviously, the morning coaching classes and studies took a hit when I was out of town.

'The commute within Delhi was by a bicycle or *phat phati* (legend has it that Harley Davidson bikes were left by the British when they departed from India. These bikes were especially popular with Allied troops during World War II. Some enterprising Indians converted these bikes into public transport vehicles, the seven- or eight-seater, three-wheel motor rickshaw, popularly known as phat phati). These phat phatis plied in Delhi's Connaught Place, Chandni Chowk and other areas. They were banned by the Supreme Court in 1998 because of their pollution levels,' QRG would describe.

With QRG settled, elders began to worry about looking for a life partner for him. Sometime in 1962, Kewal Krishna, QRG's older brother, who worked in Chandigarh, mentioned to his colleague Hukumat Rai that he was looking for a matrimonial match for his brother. Hukumat Rai said that his niece, Vinod, was of marriageable age. Why not get the two families to meet each other?

Vinod was very young, and was in no mood to get married. Still, under pressure from family, she agreed to meet QRG. Though she liked him when they met, marriage was not on her mind at all. Then her family mounted pressure in the time-tested way—it would only be possible for her two sisters to get 'settled' in life if she got married. Such were the times! She was left with no choice but to give in. The match was finalized in September 1962. QRG was twenty-five; she was seventeen.

My mother's family hailed from Patiala. The family had been in the business of selling pickles and had a shop in the local pickle market. They often supplied pickles to the Patiala royals. Her great-grandfather was fairly rich but the family wealth had been squandered away by his only son. So, my mother's father and her brothers had got into the business of Ayurveda.

There is an interesting anecdote about her childhood. When she was sixteen, a cousin's friend, who had developed an interest in palmistry, studied her palm and predicted that she would get married in one and a half years and would one day travel by air—again an improbable dream, going by the dire financial situation of the family. But every word he said ultimately came true.

That wasn't all. Sometime in 2000, she happened to meet a fortune teller in Delhi. He looked at the lines of her palm and said that she would soon be counted among the richest women in the country. Again, she laughed at him. Once again, the prediction came true! Fact is often stranger than fiction.

Meanwhile, QRG's mother, Kalawati, was diagnosed with cirrhosis of the liver. She died on 30 November 1962. On 26 February 1963, QRG and Vinod got married.

After the wedding, my mother moved in with the family at the Krishna Nagar house. A few months later, Surinderji, QRG's younger brother, got into a fight with Manoj, the landlord's son. It was a minor thing, not uncommon among young lads. But the landlord's wife took it badly. In a shrill voice, so that everybody could hear, she said, 'All they pay [as rent] is Rs 90 per month, but they behave as if they own the house.'

My mother was upset. She told QRG, in no uncertain terms, that she would not live in that house any longer. QRG understood her indignation and in November 1963 bought a house, also in Krishna Nagar, for the princely sum of Rs 18,000. It wasn't a grand house, and the walls weren't even plastered, but it was their own home. She had all of four saris, but she felt on top of the world.

The money was not great—every month QRG gave his wife Rs 800 to run the household. She was barely able to make ends meet. But she revelled in the joy of running her own home.

Ajesh, their first child and my older brother, was born in August 1965 in Patiala. As was the custom at that time, Mother had gone to her parents' place to deliver her first child.

In 1965, Lekh Raj, QRG's uncle, died in a road accident in Delhi. Between O.P. Gupta and QRG, they decided to take care of the deceased uncle's family. The family house at Malerkotla was sold and the money was given to his widow. Over the next couple of years, they also paid for the weddings of her two daughters. The family bonds were always strong.

Whenever O.P. Gupta came to Delhi, all the brothers and their children would get together for a big family meal. Their businesses may have been different, their world views may not have matched, but there were strong emotional ties that bound the family together. During those days, QRG used to travel to Bombay frequently on business, and there was one particular hotel he used to check into.

Every day, O.P. Gupta would write two identical letters from Calcutta, one to P.C. Gupta in Delhi and the other to QRG in Bombay, detailing what happened in business that day, outlining the opportunities and the threats. P.C. Gupta would send two identical letters to Calcutta and Bombay, and QRG sent one each to Delhi and Calcutta with similar details.

The three of them were always on the lookout for arbitrage possibilities—buy cheap in Bombay and sell expensive in Calcutta, for instance. The accounts for such trades were kept by O.P. Gupta in Calcutta. There was full trust between the three, and there was never any dispute. Those were simple days.

Two weddings took place in the family in 1967—Lekh Raj's second daughter and QRG's youngest sister, Sarla. The second wedding took place in May 1967, twenty days after QRG's second child, Geeta, was born. O.P. Gupta had come from Calcutta to attend the weddings.

One day during that visit, QRG confided in him that there was something bothering him.

Despite his quiet and serene life, there were rumblings in QRG's mind. There was something missing. He was ambitious and he wanted to do more. As he travelled to Bombay and Calcutta quite frequently, he realized there was scope to expand the business considerably. He wanted to set up another shop in India's financial capital. When QRG called P.C. Gupta from Bombay to discuss the idea, the latter asked him to come back immediately.

P.C. Gupta, the uncle-partner, was not interested in any expansion plans. In some ways, he was satisfied with what he had and what he earned. In a different vein, he was a pessimist. He would complain about how the business had become difficult, competition had increased with the entry of newcomers and, at the same time, old shopkeepers in Bhagirath Palace had to sell off existing businesses.

QRG was the opposite. He wanted to grow, he wanted to become big, not merely to earn more money, but to satisfy his never-ending ambition to do new things. He was a diehard optimist. He saw the potential in Bombay, Calcutta and other cities. Competition, he felt, was good since it made a trader work harder. More sellers in Bhagirath Palace meant more business because more buyers would now recognize the market as the one-stop shopping place for electrical goods.

Discontent between the two partners had been brewing for some time, though nothing untoward happened and there was no ugly outburst of passion.

One day, in 1967, QRG confronted P.C. Gupta and said this complacency and fear could not go on. P.C. Gupta did not want a change in the status quo. He replied, 'Aisa hi chalega' (it will go on like this only). When QRG suggested a separation, his uncle agreed. Obviously, they had reached a point where their differences couldn't be wished away.

QRG asked O.P. Gupta to settle the matter amicably. QRG really valued his opinion. He was like his guru and mentor, and O.P. Gupta, in turn, loved him like a son. They read the same books, liked the same films (*Mughal-e-Azam*, *Sikandar-e-Azam* and *Pukar*, to name a few) and had similar tastes in life. Both had deep faith in the teachings of the Gita and Mahatma Gandhi. Both believed in karma and found little worth in rituals.

Their tastes, too, were similar. After O.P. Gupta got a trolley on which his morning tea used to arrive, QRG got a similar contraption made for himself!

And now he wanted O.P. Gupta to iron out the differences that had emerged with P.C. Gupta.

Truth be told, QRG had no desire to sacrifice the relationship with his uncle for the sake of business. And that's how P.C. Gupta wanted to leave the business. No one fought or shouted at each other. All three of them sat down at the table, and discussed the matter over a few glasses of lassi. O.P. Gupta suggested that the best way was for one of the partners to get cash for his 50 per cent stake and the other the full ownership of the shop. Of course, whoever exited would not enter the same line of business.

To decide the price for the 50 per cent stake held by the seller, he said that either of the two could name the initial purchase price, with the second partner given the option to increase it by a factor of Rs 10,000. The informal auction could continue until one side accepted the other's offer.

P.C. Gupta started with Rs 35,000; QRG immediately upped it to Rs 45,000, and P.C. Gupta agreed to the price. That was it! The deal was struck in May 1967; QRG had to pay an initial amount of Rs 10,000 and the balance by 31 December. The trio had another round of lassi, shook hands, and the deal was done. QRG was now the sole owner of Guptajee & Co.

There was only one minor hiccup: QRG had no savings, not for the immediate payment, and definitely not for the entire amount. He only had the confidence that he could earn Rs 45,000 over the next six months because of the business opportunities he had spotted. That still left him with the task of finding Rs 10,000, which he promptly borrowed yet again from his brother-in-law, Raj Kumar. He also managed to pay the remaining amount within the deadline.

(Raj Kumar died in 1978. QRG helped his sister sell their house at Pathankot and buy one in Delhi. He trained her son, Ajay Garg, in Havells and opened a shop for him in Bhagirath Palace called K. Raj & Co. He is now a Havells dealer.)

This, in hindsight, is such a wonderful template for family separations. Rarely have Indian business families separated without acrimony. One may argue that the business was tiny when QRG and P.C. Gupta separated, and not much was at stake, but there is no reason why settlements cannot be mutually negotiated. In most other cases, families—brothers, uncle and nephew, even father and son—have washed their dirty linen in public.

QRG, in his homespun wisdom, knew that there was no point in fighting a war in which everybody bleeds financially as well as emotionally. He avoided these wars at all costs and hoped he wouldn't have to face them in the future. Unfortunately, he was wrong.

However, this split had no bearing on QRG's personal relationship with his uncle. With the money he had received, P.C. Gupta opened a machinery store in GB Road, called Gupta Engineers. Ganda Ram, his older brother, along with his son, V.P. Gupta, already had a store there called Gupta Traders. P.C. Gupta decided to follow their example. He remained a trader till his death around ten years ago.

When his daughter got married two or three years after the separation, it was QRG who did all the bandobast. During P.C. Gupta's last days, when he was stricken with cancer, a *vaid* (an Indian medicine doctor) had advised him to take cow's milk and ghee made of cow's milk. QRG ensured that the two commodities reached him every morning from his farmhouse.

P.C. Gupta's wife, who died in 2014, wrote a long booklet for QRG when he turned seventy-five. It contained her memories, bhajans and old photographs. She lavished fulsome praise on QRG, fondly remembered the days he lived with them in their house at Daryaganj, and highlighted that the separation did not weaken the bond between uncle and nephew. It was all very good.

To be fair, there was some consternation at the time of the separation in QRG's mind. After they had decided to part ways, P.C. Gupta wrote to all the business associates that he was no longer associated with Guptajee & Co. and that they should do business with it at their own risk. The communication unnerved QRG, though P.C. Gupta was only doing the right thing in his own matter-of-fact way. He had no intention to rile his nephew. Even though relations between P.C. Gupta and QRG later became amiable, this act left a mark on QRG's mind. He was now in charge of his destiny. The buck stopped with him.

FIVE

The Calcutta Connection

One of the companies that Guptajee & Co. dealt with was Fort Gloster Industries, which was owned by the Bangur family. The Bangurs were a fabulously rich Marwari family of Calcutta. There was a time when it was the fourth largest business group in the country after Tata, Birla and Mafatlal in terms of assets. And in terms of cash in hand, it was probably ahead of all the others. In our younger days, we used to hear stories of their fabulous wealth—how they would only eat off silver plates!

The family had roots in the share broking business and had diversified into manufacturing from there. Their first manufacturing venture was West Coast Paper. Subsequently, they acquired a jute mill called Fort Gloster Industries, which was listed on the stock market. Its factory was located at Bauria, a small place that fell on the railway line from Calcutta to Kharagpur.

Sometime in the early 1960s, the Bangurs decided to make cables within the compound of the jute mill at Bauria in technical collaboration with British Insulated Callender's Cables (this company was formed in 1945 by the merger of two long-established cable firms, Callender's Cable & Construction Company and British Insulated Cable). They decided to sell under the Gloster brand. One of its many dealers in Delhi was Guptajee & Co.

Its marketing manager, a gentleman called Madhav Das, had come to Delhi to meet the dealers. So far, he had dealt with P.C. Gupta, who was the external face of Guptajee & Co. Now, he would have to deal with QRG. Initially, QRG was a little apprehensive, inexperienced as he was in such matters. But all his fears proved unfounded. He hit it off with Das quite well.

One reason was that QRG was different from the other traders of Bhagirath Palace. While most of them were happy to sit behind the counter all day long and wait for customers, QRG was keen to move around and expand the market. The routine work, he felt, could just as easily be done by an employee. There was a certain restlessness in him. He would say, 'Khaaj honi chahiye' (you need to have the itch to grow and succeed).

It was Das who encouraged QRG to move around in the market and talk to customers. He suggested that QRG should buy a motorcycle. But that was an expensive proposition. Das suggested the solution—the company had one motorcycle, a Royal Enfield, which it could sell to QRG at a depreciated price. QRG agreed to this proposition immediately.

Within ten days of the separation, QRG had become the proud owner of a motorcycle. This was the first sign that QRG's fate was all set to change for the better. Money now started pouring in. A month before the separation, my sister, Geeta, had been born. She seemed to be the family's good luck charm.

Now there was no turning back. Sometime in 1968, when my mother was expecting me, QRG took her, Ajesh and Geeta somewhere on his motorcycle. Of course, they were barely able to ride comfortably. My mother began to think it was time for the family to own a car, especially since their third child was on the way. Within two or three days, QRG bought his first car—a second-hand Ambassador, the World War II model that still exists. QRG would drive it with pride on the roads of Delhi.

In 1971, my parents' car had broken down in the posh Civil Lines area, right in front of the landmark Exchange Stores near the Oberoi Maidens. While the mechanic was repairing the car, QRG and my mother decided to eat chaat. She remarked that the area looked good and wished she could stay here. In those days, this was one of the most upmarket areas of Delhi. It had huge bungalows built for imperial civilian officers after the capital was transferred from Calcutta to Delhi in 1911.

Six months later, QRG sold the Krishna Nagar house for Rs 70,000 and bought a spacious home in Civil Lines, the original abode of Delhi's rich and famous, for Rs 2,40,000. It was spread over 240 square yards.

I was born in 1969. My earliest memories of our new house are that it was big and had high ceilings. During the 1971 war, when a total blackout was ordered, I remember QRG and my uncle putting up brown paper on the light vents.

All this, of course, did not come easily. QRG worked very hard. After the separation, QRG had to first earn enough profits to pay his uncle, and also prove that his reason for the split—that the business was not growing fast enough—was genuine. Thus, he would work long hours and would frequently be away from home for days together.

On his bike, QRG would travel within and outside Delhi in search of business. One of his favourite stops was Modinagar, an industrial township on the road from Delhi to Meerut. Set up by the Modi family, then led by the patriarch Gujar Mal Modi, this was where the group made a wide range of products from hurricane lanterns to sugar and chemicals.

Modinagar was big—the Modis, at that time, were among the country's top business families. It was an industrial township with factories, colonies, schools and hospitals built by the Modis. Today, it is in a sorry state. The look of an industrial ghost town is unmistakable. But at that time, it was buzzing with activity—a temple of Modern India as Jawaharlal Nehru, the country's first prime minister, had envisioned.

QRG would drive to Modinagar in the morning, where the company would post its requirements for cables, etc. on the noticeboard. QRG would read the notices and place his bids. Then, one day, luck smiled at him.

'The Modi clan had established a new company, Modipon, in the 1960s in collaboration with Rohm & Hass of the US to make man-made yarn and fibres. I spoke to the purchase manager and visited him at Modinagar on my bike. He said the order for cables had gone to Siemens. A cheque for advance payment had also been issued to the supplier. Since, Modipon had a foreign tie-up, it wanted to give the contract to a multinational corporation. Undeterred, I asked if I could meet K.K. Modi, Gujar Mal Modi's eldest son, who was handling the commissioning of the plant. Surprisingly, my wish was granted. Within ten minutes of the conversation, Modi agreed to buy the cables from me. He immediately cancelled the Siemens order. My pitch was simple. Since I was a distributor for Fort Gloster Industries, I said that we had a foreign tie-up, our quality was as good, our delivery would be faster and, we could give him a 5 per cent discount over Siemens's price. A businessman is a businessman; Modi's eyes lit up at the mention of a discount. (For the record, Fort Gloster Industries was a domestic company.)

'Since he wanted the factory to come up fast, he insisted that I should stick to the delivery schedules. In fact, he asked me if I could airfreight the cables in case of delays. I nonchalantly said, of course, although I knew it was very expensive to transport cables by air,' QRG recounted one day. The reality was that all the cable made at Bauria could be moved only by road and rail.

Still, QRG stuck to the price and delivery schedules. The confidence in being able to bag such deals—Modipon's order was worth Rs 1–2 lakh—made QRG hungry for more. He also realized that it was not impossible to deal with people in a position of power.

Right from the late fifties, when QRG became an equal partner in Guptajee & Co., he grabbed opportunities by the horns, and took several calculated risks, some of which seemed like gambles.

His business now grew by leaps and bounds. Fort Gloster Industries, in due course, made QRG its sole agent for the whole of north India. Apart from Fort Gloster Industries, he became the north India distributor for Bentex, too, which made switchgears.

'After 1967, *business apne aap badhta gaya; caravan chalta gaya, caravan badhta gaya*' (business grew on its own; the caravan kept rolling and expanding), QRG would reminisce fondly about his first taste of success.

This was the time he took firm steps to ensure that his children got a good education. For Ajesh, he had St Xavier's at Civil Lines, the best school in Delhi till the eighties, in mind. This is where P.C. Gupta's son used to study. Many people told QRG that he would not be able to secure admission for his son because it only accepted 'brilliant students'. But that didn't deter QRG. He found a Goan couple, Mr and Mrs Braganza, who could teach English to his children. The couple lived in north Delhi. Mrs Braganza specialized in preparing students for school admissions. Mr Braganza used to give private lessons. He would come to our home for many years to teach us the language.

The problem was that the admissions for the season were over. Outstanding salesman that he was, QRG persisted till the school agreed to take Ajesh in. For Geeta, he chose Presentation Convent in Chandni Chowk. Both the schools were in great demand those days. He wanted only the best education for his children.

Once Ajesh was firmly ensconced in St Xavier's, it was easy for QRG to get me admitted to the same school a few years later. That Ajesh was an outstanding student made it that much easier for me. When I went for the interview, QRG had instructed me to say whatever I liked. I was fond of singing and was hoping that I would be asked to show off my vocal skills. But the fathers and nuns on the interview panel had no such intention. So, after the interview, I asked Father Saldanha, the principal, if I could sing. He nodded and I sang '*Hum chhupe rustam hain . . .*' which was the title song of Dev Anand's 1973 film, *Chhupa Rustam.*

Did success and money change QRG? Not one bit. The fact is, during the period when he was in his mid to late twenties, his desire to become an entrepreneur was driven by non-materialistic factors.

Call it ambition, call it passion or call it natural instincts. But QRG was a businessman because he wanted to be in business. Personal wealth was a small consideration; there was much more to being a businessman. This was before he met any of the leading businessmen of the day. But he knew that they wouldn't have become big if they were driven only by the personal profit motive.

Right from the beginning, when he was a small trader, QRG understood that the above two arguments were only two sides of the capitalist coin. Greed was good, but only if it was corporate greed, i.e. greed to become big, greed to expand, greed for growth. It was personal greed and personal wealth that he abhorred.

This antagonism against materialistic wants and display evolved into a philosophy of ethical management by the time he turned into a manufacturer. Let us not forget that the 1960s and 1970s had a distinct anti-business environment. Personal and corporate taxes on business persons were high; the government also imposed a high wealth tax.

Most businesses, including traders, believed in evading, not just avoiding, taxes. Many sold goods off the books to generate black money, which flew into foreign tax havens, and did not pay the taxes due to the government. Traders routinely procured duplicates, and sold them as originals, to make higher profits, most of which were not disclosed in their balance sheets. It was an era marked by lack of business values.

Even in that environment, QRG remained rooted in ethics. In fact, one of his favourite anecdotes is of fellow traders in Bhagirath Palace, who would deride him for not dealing in the black market. QRG would counter them, 'How can you conduct all your business in cash?'

Those years also helped QRG discover the salesman in him. He could be very persuasive when the occasion demanded. The environment in which he lived as a child shaped him as a person and as a businessman. He may not have realized this as a child, but it laid the moral, ethical, philosophical, spiritual and practical foundation that later helped him build Havells into a $3-billion empire.

It was the socio-politico-religious environment that shaped him during the first ten years of his life. QRG was born near Malerkotla. In the pre-Independence period it was ruled by the Pathan Afghans, who claimed to have descended from the Lodhi dynasty.

QRG's name, Qimat, and the fact that it starts with Q and not K, owes its origins to the Islamic rule and Muslim majority in the region. An indication of the community strength in Malerkotla can be gauged from the fact that all ten candidates in the constituency, who stood for the 2012 assembly elections, were Muslims.

During Partition, when the Indian subcontinent was divided into India and Pakistan, and even later, Malerkotla witnessed peaceful coexistence between Muslims, Sikhs and Hindus. There were no communal riots, and the area was hailed as 'an island of peace where brotherhood is handed down as tradition'.

A study by Anna Bigelow, North Carolina University, concluded 'throughout this [Partition] trauma, Malerkotla became known as a safe zone for Muslims travelling towards Pakistan'.

She added 'during subsequent (post-Independence) periods of communal tensions in India, Malerkotla has transcended tensions and overcome the strains of violent events such as the destruction of the Babri Masjid in Ayodhya in 1992 or the riots in Gujarat in 2002'.

Despite these important phases of secular peace, the region was engulfed in communal tensions at several junctures. Biglow concluded that despite the Guru Gobind Singh incident, there were several clashes between the Muslim and Sikh rulers during the region's existence as a princely state (1454–1948).

Even between 1935 and 1941, when QRG was born, the Hindus and Muslims fought each other over religious matters. The six-year period of religious skirmishes started with a Hindu katha in a building that overlooked a mosque.

Therefore, during his young days, until his eleventh year (1937–48), QRG witnessed both sides of the communal equation—tensions and harmony. He saw the riots between Hindus and Muslims in his early years, but no one died in 1947–48 (Partition), when north India and neighbouring Pakistan were drenched with blood and were full of bodies.

These incidents made him secular and accommodative to contradictory religious and social viewpoints. They ingrained in him the ability to try and understand other people, even if they were different, and listen to them. It is a trait that later helped him in business.

After he came to Delhi, and became a partner in Guptajee & Co., he travelled across north, east and west India. His style was the same, whether he spoke to a seller or buyer. He wanted to be seen as a friend, as someone who had come to transact a fair deal.

'I did not take much time to adjust to city life, or to the manner in which business was conducted in the cities. The basics were the same,' QRG would say.

For QRG, it was important to show his honesty, integrity, fairness and earnestness. He always remembered an elderly trader in Bombay, whose surname was Rawal and whom everyone called Guruji, who disliked QRG in those initial days. Guruji operated out of Lohar Chawl market which, like Bhagirath Palace, was the wholesale market for electrical goods in Bombay.

'Guruji had some animosity towards Delhi traders, as did many others in Bombay. They believed that we did not have business ethics and we were keen to cheat them. One of the reasons for this attitude was the nature of traders of automobile components in Delhi's Kashmiri Gate. They used to mostly sell duplicate components as original. Even now, the area is infamous for spurious parts. So, he refused to deal with me or entertain me. He told me in no uncertain terms that he didn't deal with Dilliwalas.

'A bit angry and a bit frustrated, I did not visit Guruji's shop for months. However, I made sure I acted with other traders in Lohar Chawl in the best possible manner—in the same ethical way that I did elsewhere. Slowly, but surely, I built a reputation as a fair trader, someone who would not cheat and who would keep his word. After two or three months, as I passed by Guruji's shop, he called me and said,

"I did not know that you were different from other Delhi traders." Although I was happy with his comment, and he was a respected trader in Lohar Chawl, I still retorted that he should not paint everyone from the capital with the same brush.

'Guruji and I became friends; the relationship lasted till he died,' QRG recalled.

In May 1968, barely a year after QRG separated from his uncle and took control of the electrical goods shop in Delhi's Bhagirath Palace, he found that the adjacent shop, owned by a film distributor, was up for sale. He did not have the money to buy it, but in his heart he knew that he may not get such a chance again.

'I realized that there were only limited shops in the market, and an opportunity to buy another one would be rare. Also, I felt that the purchase would enable me to grow the business. I spoke to the broker, who fixed the price at Rs 35,000,' remembered QRG.

In a few minutes, the broker said the seller had raised the asking price to Rs 40,000. To finalize the deal, QRG paid him a *biyana* (advance) of Rs 5000 and told him that he should not increase the price again. His instructions to the broker were to not come back without sealing the deal. However, the broker came back and said that he had bought it on his behalf for Rs 45,000. Though the price had gone up by Rs 10,000 in just half an hour, QRG bought the shop.

'My father, who managed the shop with me, was there when the deal was closed. He asked, "Qimat, what are you doing? How will we raise such a big amount?" I answered, "If I spend this money, I am sure God will find ways to send it to me." I know I was being audacious. But in my mind there was no uncertainty; I knew the second shop had to do well. I had just tied the knot, and had a large family and parents to support, but my wife backed me,' QRG would recall happily.

'*Okhal main sir dal diya to mooslo se kya darna,*' QRG would often say. If you have taken up a work, don't let a blow or two knock you off your course. This would remain a lifelong philosophy for QRG—and for Havells.

Life was set to change for him once again.

SIX

Buying Havells

Jhang, now in Pakistan, is where the tragic love story of Heer and Ranjha played out.

It traces its history to 2000 BCE when it was known as Jhang Sial. At the time of Partition, Muslims formed the majority of the district's population, and so it chose to become a part of Pakistan. The Hindus and Sikhs left the homes they had lived in and the farms they had tilled for generations to trudge to India. Many settled in Punjab and Haryana, and some made their way to Delhi.

Among those who made Delhi their home was Haveli Ram Gandhi. A native of Chiniot in the Jhang district, he must have been a businessman of sorts before Partition, and did not waste much time getting started once again in life. In 1948, he registered a brand called Havell's (The brand was actually Havell's. It was only in 2008 that we changed it to Havells.)

There is some confusion about how he chose the name. One story is that 'Havells' was derived from his own name, Haveli. The other is that Haveli Ram, or one of his loyalists or family members saw the name in Europe—there was a

Belgian company called Havells—and suggested it since it was similar to Haveli's name. Another story goes that he used to import electrical products from a Dutch company called Havells. Maybe it was a combination of all three. The fact is that even today most consumers feel that Havells is a foreign brand.

I never met him, but over the years I have heard numerous stories about him—some good, some tragic. It seems he was an astrologer and could make accurate predictions. He was close to his wife and used to consider her his good luck charm. In the fifties, Haveli Ram started Havells Electrical Sales Corporation. Some old-timers have told me that the enterprise was launched in 1956.

Initially, Haveli Ram, like most traders in India, imported several electrical products like switchgears, starters and meters, rebranded them as Havells, and sold them in the market. These products were not made in India; Larsen & Toubro, one of the giants in switchgears, started local production only in the sixties. Most imports came from the Eastern European nations as well as from West Germany and Holland.

By 1962–63, the market for imports changed dramatically. Morarji Desai, then the country's finance minister, explained the changed environment in his 1963 Budget speech. 'The one sector of our economy which has been the cause of the greatest concern to me throughout the year is our external payments situation. The summer of 1962 witnessed a sharp deterioration in our foreign exchange reserves . . . we had, therefore, to make further cuts in import quotas already announced . . .' he told Parliament.

A clampdown on imports meant that like his counterparts, Haveli Ram found it difficult to run his business. He had only three options: (a) scale down the business or even shut it down; (b) source the products locally, though there were very few suppliers; or (c) manufacture them in-house under the Havells name.

Haveli Ram chose the last option. He set up a factory in Faridabad. Those who had seen the factory would say it was of a good standard. The machines were modern and efficient. It must have been a landmark in its own right because the place came to be called Havells Chowk. Many years later, we too would start a factory at Havells Chowk!

All seemed to be going well for Haveli Ram. Havells switches were selling briskly; in fact, there came a time when they could be found in most Delhi homes, offices and commercial establishments.

The family lived in great style in Golf Links, the luxurious residential colony in central Delhi. By one account, Haveli Ram paid income tax of Rs 38 lakh in one of his more prosperous years. Though taxation rates were high then, it points to substantial riches.

Then tragedy struck Haveli Ram: his wife, who had brought him great luck, died. Somebody who was once close to the family insisted that Haveli Ram knew beforehand the day she was to die. Once she passed way, he lost all his zest for life.

Haveli Ram then asked his son, Anil (my namesake), to come back from London and handle the business. But Anil could not manage it well. He could not adjust to life in Delhi. He sought solace in parties and socializing, but that too didn't help. He finally committed suicide in 1976.

Because of all this, the quality of Havells products fell consistently. There came a time in the late sixties when the company was blacklisted by several government departments. Its brand equity was down. The company was gasping for oxygen.

Enter Inder Matta.

Matta worked in the marketing department of Asian Cables, which was owned by the Goenka family of Calcutta. He would often do the rounds of Bhagirath Palace to find dealers who could stock his products as well. This is where he met QRG. After the split with P.C. Gupta, Guptajee & Co. was growing at a fast pace; so, making QRG a dealer was important for Matta.

Matta had come to know that Fort Gloster Industries gave QRG a discount of 20 per cent on its listed price, of which 12 per cent was passed on to his customers; so, he offered him a 35 per cent discount. This was an opportunity to make substantially higher profits, but QRG didn't yield to the temptation. He was committed to his relationship with Fort Gloster Industries.

Most dealers would have taken the inducement offered by Matta. But QRG never took a short-term view of things. He was ready to forsake short-term profits, even if they were large, in order to maintain good relations with his suppliers. This was to be a lifelong trait.

One day, Matta, after another unsuccessful round of talks with QRG, was exiting Bhagirath Palace when he was accosted by a man who ran a small tea stall under a staircase, not far from where Guptajee & Co. was located. He pleaded with Matta to make him a dealer. Somehow, Matta agreed. The vendor was in business the very next day.

Naturally, this hurt Guptajee & Co.'s business, and QRG ticked off Matta about it. But, I think, he saw that Matta was just doing his job and therefore held no grudge against him. Over time, they even became friends.

Guptajee & Co. had begun to stock Havells products in 1969. A few years later, when Matta's wife was battling for life in a Delhi hospital, QRG gave him his car to run around for help, while he chose to move around in an autorickshaw.

In 1969 or so, Matta left Asian Cables to get into business himself. After a year, he joined Havells. His job was to be present at the Gandhi household at Golf Links in the morning. Anil Gandhi would get up around noon. Then Matta would take him to the Havells office at Asaf Ali Road in Daryaganj for a few hours. In the evening, Anil Gandhi would do the rounds of the various hotels in town, and have dinner at one of them. After dropping him home, Matta would finally call it a day.

There was a large government order that companies like Havells were chasing in Chandigarh. In fact, Havells was fairly confident of bagging it, and had already started production to execute the order. Unfortunately, it didn't get the order. This landed the company in a soup. It appears that Matta sold a large chunk of this unsold stock to QRG.

But QRG couldn't sell it on. His money was stuck—something a trader doesn't like one bit. He wanted to return the stock to Havells and get his money back. This plunged Havells into a deeper crisis. Then, one day, Matta came with a message—would QRG like to buy Havells and settle the accounts?

QRG was interested. The company had a brand, though there were quality problems. It also had a factory. Perhaps, as a trader, QRG knew that the real profit margins were in manufacturing, not in trading. If he missed this chance, he felt, all his life he would only collect the commission other manufacturers shared with him. Fort Gloster Industries gave him 2 per cent commission on cables and 5 per cent on wires. The bulk of its business was, of course, the low-margin cables.

Haveli Ram asked for Rs 7 lakh for the company, which included the factory. This was more than QRG could rustle up. So, he involved three others to invest in the venture—his uncles O.P. Gupta and P.C. Gupta, and his older brother, Kewal Krishna, who had given up his job in Chandigarh and got into the machine parts business at GB Road. He proposed that each would contribute 25 per cent for the acquisition, and hence own 25 per cent of the company, though he would manage it after the acquisition.

Initially, everybody agreed. But the next day, two people backed out—P.C. Gupta and Kewal Krishna. They probably didn't have the appetite to take this risk. Seeing their enthusiasm wane, O.P. Gupta also opted out but encouraged QRG to go for it on his own.

Now that he couldn't rustle up the cash, QRG offered to buy just the brand and the trademark—not the factory at Faridabad. Meanwhile, another Bhagirath Palace dealer called Charanjit Singh, had got wind of the negotiation and joined the fray. Finally, QRG bagged it. The money he paid was less than the Rs 7 lakh Haveli Ram had asked for in the initial deal. Havells now belonged to QRG!

He expanded it, and how! At the time of QRG's demise in 2014, the market cap of Havells was Rs 18,000 crore. Out of that, physical assets were just Rs 1500 crore or so; the rest was the brand value of Havells. In other words, from 1971 to 2014, he drove the worth of the brand from a few lakhs to Rs 16,500 crore!

'Despite my trading years, I was still young and scared of any invisible liability attached to the factory. I did not understand the dynamics and nuances of buying a company. Also, I was short on cash,' QRG would remember in his later years. 'I gave Haveli Ram an alternative. Let me buy the brand and goodwill minus the physical assets. Haveli Ram agreed and said that he would sell the plant separately and exit the electrical goods business. I got Havells.'

QRG knew very well that in those days he had probably done the unthinkable. 'No trader would have thought along those lines. What I did was nothing short of a miracle. No one attached much value in the seventies to brand value, intellectual property and brand goodwill. Such concepts in management lexicon came later.' The concept of the brand as a source of real value was not established even in the western nations then.

In fact, what QRG did was nothing short of commercial sacrilege; no businessman would have done it at that time.

To put it in context, it was in 1996 that Ratan Tata, the former chairman of Tata Sons, asked his operational companies (Tata Steel, Tata Motors and others) to pay an annual royalty to Tata Sons, the holding company, which owned the brand, for the privilege of using the 'Tata' brand.

Remember, those were the days of the Licence Raj. The focus was on production. It was the government that made projections of supply and demand, and accordingly handed out production licences. Whatever was produced got sold. Later, it was found that every business house would simply sit on a large number of unused licences to create shortages and drive up prices—the complications of a command economy. In such a scenario, there was no need for anybody to focus on brands.

Most businesses therefore were production-oriented. Remember that this was also the time India refused to acknowledge product patents. Intellectual property rights were viewed with disapproval as anti-people. To take this contrarian call was a bold move on QRG's part. It shows he had the two traits that make a pioneer: the spirit of adventure and unassailable self-belief.

To make sense of QRG's decision, one has to understand his business mindset as well as his instinctive abilities and his courage. I say courage because Havells was blacklisted by several departments. It is easy to buy a well-managed asset, but to buy an asset that is not doing too well and turn it around needs tremendous guts and conviction.

In 1971, QRG was a trader who wanted to become an even bigger trader. He had seen his counterparts start brands which expanded furiously. Bentex was an example of high growth through procurement of electrical products from third parties and rebranding them under its own name. 'I thought I could do what Bentex and others had done. I could use Havells, and extend the brand to other product categories,' QRG told an interviewer many years later.

Also, the opportunity was presented and QRG was quick enough to grab it. This was a common theme throughout his entrepreneurial career. He could spot opportunities, gauge their potential and then jump headlong into the new situations with full confidence, even when everyone around him was unsure. He had foresight and the courage of conviction.

Having bought the brand and not the factory, QRG wanted to do what other traders had done—outsource products and sell under their house label. Over the next few years, Havells Industries, a new partnership firm, grew in this fashion.

QRG would maintain cordial relations with Haveli Ram, though there was one hiccup. Anil, Haveli Ram's son, had revived a defunct company called Havells Private Ltd in partnership with another businessman. Many years later, we found that this company too was selling under the Havells brand. The matter went to the courts, which stayed him from using the brand name and trademark. He then began to sell under another brand (HPL).

I remember that in subsequent years, QRG would be sad when he came back from his meetings with Haveli Ram because he had fallen on hard times. He could never recover the losses in business. A few years after he sold Havells, Haveli Ram lost his son, Anil. This pushed him further into despair.

According to one account that I have heard, Haveli Ram had started drinking heavily which took a toll on his health. His family, in the interest of his health, had forbidden him from drinking. During one of his last visits, Haveli Ram asked QRG for Rs 100 to buy a drink. He died in 1981. It was a sad end to a rollercoaster life.

(Anil's son is the famous fashion designer Rohit Gandhi. I have met him on a few occasions.)

Meanwhile at Guptajee & Co., QRG cemented his ties further with Fort Gloster Industries. In 1972, QRG became the sole selling agent of the company for Delhi. To complete the legal formalities, he travelled to Calcutta where he met Shri Niwas Bangur, the son of the patriarch, Narsing Dass Bangur.

After the meeting, Shri Niwas Bangur suggested that QRG should meet his father the next morning. But QRG had booked himself on the evening flight to Delhi, which had cost him Rs 500—not an insignificant amount of money at that time. He decided to stay on in Calcutta.

In life, he concluded, such things do happen; one has to account for such unforeseen expenses while growing one's business. QRG never let short-term problems or minor pitfalls make him lose sight of the bigger goal.

His visits to Calcutta now became more frequent. Of course, he had a base there to stay—the house of his favourite uncle, O.P. Gupta. I remember those visits because on his return, QRG used to bring imported toys for me, bought at the famous Kidderpore Market. I used to be sick quite a lot at that time, so something or the other would come for me on every visit. In 1975, he took the whole family to Calcutta— that was the first time we three siblings travelled by air.

QRG had this unique ability to observe and imbibe good habits and practices from people he met. His antenna was always up. The Bangurs were such people. Their office was at Chowringhee Road, while they lived at Alipore. It was said that if a bird flew into their home, it would come back with gold in its beak—such was their fabled wealth.

Much of QRG's interaction was with Shri Niwas Bangur. He was a God-fearing man. QRG learnt simplicity and straightforwardness from him. He observed keenly how Shri Niwas Bangur gave importance to his dealers and agents. Today, dealer incentives are huge. They are taken on extended overseas vacations and given expensive gifts. At that time, the relationship was driven by the promoter's personal touch.

Later, at Havells, people would often wonder at the strong bonds between QRG and the dealers. He not only knew all the dealers personally but would also keep himself informed of their children's progress. Many of them would tell him their private problems and seek his advice, which he gave in all sincerity.

In any brand-oriented business, the dealer is the key. It is the dealer who controls where and when the product changes hands. A bad word from the dealer can kill a product and ruin the business. That's why it is essential to keep the dealers happy. The commission is important but it can be matched by your rivals; what makes the difference is the personal touch. He was also impressed with the way Shri Niwas Bangur dealt with employees—they were like family for him. He would trust them fully and would keep no secrets from them. After a task was assigned, he would give them full freedom to execute it. This, QRG quickly realized, was the best way to handle a large business. If the promoter starts doing everything himself, he will be left with a bunch of dispirited employees, which can be suicidal for the organization.

Those who joined the Bangurs only left the group on retirement. Such was their reputation as employers.

P.R. Mehta, who joined Fort Gloster Industries in 1975 as a deputy to Madhav Das, would share several interesting anecdotes about the Bangurs.

In those days, sales and marketing deals were usually struck over drinks. That was the culture of the times. Mehta, who had joined from Apar Cables, was told by his superior, Madhav Das, over drinks, that the Bangurs did not like people who drank. So he would have to drink on the sly and be discreet about it.

Mehta, who would later become a devout Krishna follower and give up alcohol completely, found it irksome. 'Entertainment' was an inalienable part of marketing. Barely a week into the job, he barged into Shri Niwas Bangur's office and said that he needed to talk—urgently. At that time, another senior executive was in the room. As that executive began to leave, Shri Niwas Bangur asked him to stay. 'You can speak freely in front of him,' he told Mehta. *'Ye toh gharan ke log hain'* (he is family).

(This was meant to make the executive feel important. I have often wondered about the extraordinary openness and transparency QRG institutionalized at Havells—where did it come from? Maybe, QRG learnt it all from the Bangurs.)

Mehta blurted it all out. It was not possible, he said, to concoct bills every time he drank. And, he told Shri Niwas Bangur who was by now shell-shocked that he imbibed whiskey almost every single evening. After a while, Shri Niwas Bangur recovered and said to the executive in Marwari, 'What difference does it make to me?'

Shri Niwas Bangur was being practical. Why should his puritanism hinder the work of his employees? Mehta came out of the meeting relieved.

QRG had the same attitude towards such issues. He didn't force his personal choices on others. While he was a teetotaller, he wouldn't stop others from drinking. Even after we had grown up, there was no official ban on drinking. I am sure it wouldn't have offended him if we drank a glass or two of wine. That we chose not to drink at all was a different matter.

During the seventies and eighties, the cable industry had an informal association that would meet late into the night. Everybody except QRG would drink. But QRG would be in the swing of things like everybody else. He did this to ensure that others didn't feel awkward in his company. He certainly knew how to win friends.

QRG would frequently, and openly, acknowledge his debt to the Bangurs. 'From the several meetings I had with Shri Niwas Bangur, and other managers in Fort Gloster Industries, I learnt the tricks of management. How to delegate responsibilities to the managers; how to run businesses through separate departments and divisions; how to implant processes, etc. By observing them and through discussions, I gained a fair bit of knowledge of how to grow from a trader to a manufacturer.

'I understood the dynamics of manufacturing. Sometimes, I would think that if the Bangurs have done it, why can't I do it? Everyone has to start from scratch,' QRG would say.

I got to meet Narsing Dass Bangur in 1977. We had gone on a short family vacation to Pushkar in the Ajmer district of Rajasthan. It has several temples, including a rare one devoted to Brahma, and is a place of pilgrimage for devout Hindus. It so happened, Narsing Dass Bangur too was at one of the temples when we went there. We touched his feet, as QRG had instructed, and he gave us his blessings. I remember he was wearing a simple dhoti and kurta. At that time, I was keener to scrutinize his Chevrolet Impala which was parked outside.

A few years later, Ajesh and I had gone to Calcutta for a school trip. QRG had instructed us to go and meet Shri Niwas Bangur, which we dutifully did. Subsequently, when one of Shri Niwas Bangur's sons, Shreekant, came to Delhi, QRG asked us to show him around. Till then, we had only heard stories of how they ate only off silver plates, and were pleasantly surprised when he had chaat with us in Bengali Market!

Impressed with QRG's work, Fort Gloster Industries made him the sole selling agent for states like Punjab, Haryana and Himachal Pradesh in the mid-seventies, apart from Delhi. Soon, QRG had become the largest dealer in India. Out of its annual turnover of Rs 50 crore or so, almost 10 per cent came from Guptajee & Co. As most of its business was in cables, the 2 per cent commission for Guptajee & Co. would have meant an annual income of Rs 10 to 15 lakh—not small for a Bhagirath Palace trader in those times.

One day, when QRG was sitting with Shri Niwas Bangur in his office in Calcutta, an artist walked in with a dozen or so watercolours. These were paintings of deities, and looked much similar to calendar art that appears simple but conveys mythological details. There was one painting that Shri Niwas Bangur rejected but QRG liked it and asked if he could buy it instead. Shri Niwas Bangur saw no reason to object.

It's an evocative work of art—it shows Vishnu on Seshnag, surrounded by the whole pantheon of gods—Shankar, Hanuman, Saraswati, Garuda and Narad. The painting, QRG believed, changed his luck for the better. He got it framed and hung it in his office, where it still stays. It invariably catches the eye of visitors. Years later, QRG gifted a replica of it to Vickyji, O.P. Gupta's son.

Being an agent was not easy. The largest buyers of cable were various government departments. And they didn't walk up to you with orders—it was your job to sell your products to them.

India won the bid to host the Asian Games in 1982. The first edition of the games was held in Delhi in 1951. After a gap of thirty-one years, the city got the chance to play host for the second time. In the intervening years, the Asian Games had become much bigger. India too was keen to make a statement to the world.

Indira Gandhi, then prime minister, gave her elder son, Rajiv, who had so far eschewed politics and had been content to be a pilot with Air India, the job to oversee the preparations. This was perhaps her way to break him into public life.

This gave a huge boost to construction in the city—in terms of hotels, roads, flyovers, stadiums, etc. There were good business opportunities for Guptajee & Co.

In 1981, the Delhi Electricity Supply Undertaking (DESU) needed a special cable which had till date not been manufactured in India. DESU had therefore, more or less, made up its mind to import it. For Fort Gloster Industries, this was a prestigious order to chase. If it could bag it, the perception of its technological capabilities would increase manifold, which could help it get more high-value orders in the future. That's why it had tied up with Sumitomo of Japan for this project.

As Guptajee & Co. was its sole selling agent, it was natural for QRG to get involved. Since the order was important, Fort Gloster Industries had stationed Mehta and a team from Sumitomo at the Taj Mahal Hotel for months together.

QRG used to go there regularly to strategize with them. One evening, Mehta asked QRG to bring my mother and me along for dinner. Both of us went. That was the first time I ate at a five-star hotel. I was particularly awestruck when food was brought on a trolley.

In spite of their best efforts, DESU decided to import the cable.

In a last-ditch effort to salvage the deal, QRG went to meet the DESU chairman, a bureaucrat. At the meeting, he told QRG that it was an important project and he could not take the risk of sourcing substandard cable. This is when QRG said that, as a bureaucrat, had he been in the Directorate General of Technical Development, he would have done just the opposite and recommended the cable made by Fort Gloster Industries!

QRG had played on his nationalistic pride. The trick worked. He asked QRG to wait for an hour, at the end of which he handed over the prestigious contract to him. Needless to say, QRG as well as the Bangurs, were ecstatic.

Over time, Guptajee & Co. became the agent for other companies like Cutler Hammer and English Electric (it was later acquired by General Electric), but Fort Gloster Industries was its bread and butter. One day in the not too distant future, Guptajee & Co. would be eclipsed by Havells.

SEVEN

Lesson from Kanpur

In the beginning, the going at Havells was far from easy. Actually, at that time, Guptajee & Co. kept QRG very busy. In the morning and evening, he would go to meet people, mostly officers of various government departments, to get orders for cables made by Fort Gloster Industries. At that time, the culture of kickbacks was not prevalent. A lot depended on personal equations. And QRG left no stone unturned in this effort.

Of course, he had some help. My mother's elder brother, Surjitji, had come to Delhi in 1965. At the time, QRG was still running Guptajee & Co. in partnership with his uncle, P.C. Gupta. He thought there could be an interesting opportunity in automobile components. Unlike present times when all parts are sold through service centres, people would then buy parts in the open market and get the neighbourhood mechanic to fix their vehicles. So, QRG encouraged his brother-in-law, Surjitji, to set up a shop for automobile parts.

The components business was centred round Kashmiri Gate, the place where the British breached the defences of the mutineers during the 1857 revolt. Surjitji set up a shop there called Gupta Bhai & Co. in January 1966.

For about two years, he tried his best to make a success of it but the business failed to pick up. Eventually, in 1968, he closed the venture and started working for Guptajee & Co.

In 1971, after QRG had bought the Havells brand, he gifted a 27 per cent stake each to Surjitji and his younger brother, Surinderji, in Havells Industries. That's how he took care of the family. A more selfless deed would be difficult to find in the world of business.

For almost a year after buying Havells, QRG ran the business from Guptajee & Co., shop number 1831, at Bhagirath Palace. Then he took on another space at Bhagirath Palace—shop number 1826—for which he paid a *pagri*, or a deposit to the landlord. That was the first office of Havells—about 600 square feet on the ground floor and an equal space in the basement. Apart from Surinderji and Surjitji, there were a few others to help QRG in the task of running Havells.

QRG had the brand but he needed products to put the brand and the logo on. He did two things. First, he sourced switchgears from Kenbar & Co., a unit owned by Baldev Raj Kanwar in Badarpur (it subsequently relocated to Okhla). Second, he began to assemble small quantities at home.

Our home at Civil Lines was built on stilts. On the ground floor, he started the assembly. For this, he had hired more than a dozen men and women. Value addition was minimal. Drums, around which cable was wrapped, were turned on to their sides and converted into tables upon which the workers assembled the iron switches. QRG also hired some space at Grand Hotel, a dilapidated building close to our home, in order to expand the assembling operations.

The blacklisting in government departments hampered business and so sales were indifferent. All the dealers QRG met were reluctant to stock Havells products.

Then fate intervened.

One day, QRG was travelling by train and happened to meet a dealer from Kanpur. The man used to stock switches made by Siemens and Larsen & Toubro and had not entertained entreaties from QRG to display Havells switches for some time. He told QRG, rather derisively, 'Do you think you can sell whatever you want? Go and worry about manufacturing first.'

Most others would have become disheartened. QRG saw it as an invaluable message—if he had to address the quality concerns, he had no option but to get into fully fledged manufacturing.

Havells's first factory came up in 1976 at Kirti Nagar in west Delhi, now home to hundreds of furniture shops, where switchgears were assembled. The cost of the machinery for the unit was Rs 1–2 lakh, and the monthly rent for the factory was Rs 8000.

Many of QRG's friends and family members thought he had lost his mind. 'I convinced my father. My Calcutta-based uncle O.P. Gupta blessed my decision to get into manufacturing. Therefore, I could go ahead with my plan,' QRG would remember. He always liked to do things after consulting elders, especially the people whose judgement he valued.

In retrospect, it seems providential that QRG took the decisions he did during the seventies—there couldn't be a more opportune time. It was possibly the right time to buy a brand and expand business through outsourcing, rather than through manufacturing.

In March 1971, Indira Gandhi had romped back to political power when her faction of the Congress bagged 352 seats, much more than it had in 1967.

She swept to power on her election slogan 'Garibi hatao' (remove poverty) and the nationalization wave. The mood in 1971 was anti-business but pro-traders. The Bangladesh war in December that year proved profitable for traders. Most importantly, the victory in the war gave the pro-Left, pro-Soviet Indira Gandhi the confidence to pursue her own political and economic agenda. What followed was rapid nationalization, most notably in the banking sector.

By 1976, when we set up the Kirti Nagar unit, the nation's mood towards business, and also Indira Gandhi's ideology, had started changing. It was the period of the Emergency, which wreaked social and political havoc but encouraged manufacturing.

In fact, the mood during the Emergency turned against traders who were seen as hoarders and became somewhat pro-manufacturers. Dark as that time was, some things changed for the better. Bureaucrats became more efficient, trains ran on time and entrepreneurs found it easier to get clearances and transport their goods.

This is reflected by one of the diplomatic cables sent by the American embassy in New Delhi to Washington during that period. The cable, dated 22 October 1975, revealed the mindset of Indira Gandhi and her key aides on economic issues.

In it P.N. Dhar, Indira Gandhi's principal secretary at that time, told the American ambassador, William Saxbe, that there was a rightward swing in economic policies during the Emergency. Dhar reportedly argued 'against populist policies and the practice of paying bonuses to employees of loss-making companies and nationalizing sick companies, which drained out [the government's] funds'. This description of a shift in the economic philosophy, from socialism to pro-business, must have been music to the ears of the business community.

Over the next few years, QRG set up more factories in Delhi. In 1979, a second factory came up at Badli. He had bought this piece of land for Rs 1.5 lakh with the intention of putting up a warehouse to stock Fort Gloster products. Instead, he set up a second switchgear unit with an investment of Rs 12–13 lakh. A third unit came up the year after that in Tilak Nagar to make electric meters—for industrial and residential usage.

But setting up a factory wasn't an end in itself. In order to churn out good-quality products day after day, one requires good technical people. V.P. Mahendroo, one of the owners of Standard Electricals, which was a very big name in the business at that time, visited Havells's office one day and encouraged QRG to hire more engineers.

His advice appealed to QRG and so over the next few months he hired top-notch professionals from big companies like GEC, Standard Electric and Siemens to work for him. The family was scrupulously kept out of the operations. He knew that production of high-quality equipment required specialists, and it would be unwise to entrust the delicate job to a family member. In fact, he brought quite a few stars to Havells during that time—K.K. Gupta from Standard Electric and V.K. Janweja from GEC, among others.

He knew Havells was a smaller company, so he would have to pay a substantial premium to get them to work for him. But he didn't flinch. Again, he was thinking long term. Without these people, he would not have been able to produce high-quality equipment. Apart from money, QRG also showed them a clear growth path within Havells.

The sales pitch never failed. Over time, several industry veterans became a part of the Havells rolls.

But the perception of poor quality, a carry-over from the past, was not easy to shed. Once manufacturing was under control, QRG and his men focused on quality certifications. They would go over the technical details of the products with customers and explain to them that Havells's quality was second to none.

Once QRG was confident that all quality snags had been fixed and all quality certificates were obtained, he decided to make a big splash of it.

In 1980, he decided to host over 200 people at the Taj Mahal Hotel where his team would answer all quality-related questions. Among the guests were technical people from almost every government department that needed to buy switchgear or electric meters—DESU, Military Engineering Services, Delhi Vidyut Board, New Delhi Municipal Corporation et al. Also present were private buyers like factory owners and builders. A few representatives of the Directorate General of Technical Development could also be seen in the crowd.

After the introductory remarks, QRG opened the floor for a candid no-holds-barred interactive session. To answer the queries of the guests, he had seated Surjitji, Janweja and K.K. Gupta on the dais. Though the technical stuff escaped me—I was only eleven at the time—I enjoyed watching the spectacle of it all. Questions flew thick and fast but were answered competently by the three gentlemen on the dais.

By the time it ended, the mood in the crowd was upbeat. It was clear that all the doubts they had in their minds about the quality of Havells's products had dissipated. After this event, the popular perception of Havells began to change. In no time, it was off all blacklists.

At the time, Havells had an annual turnover of Rs 1 crore. For QRG to hold an event in an upmarket five-star hotel was a bold move. If you assume the cost of hosting was Rs 500 per guest, he had blown almost 1 per cent of the turnover in a matter of hours! But he knew the benefits would far outweigh the cost in the long term.

During this time, QRG was fighting a personal battle. Sometime in 1975, when he was thirty-eight, QRG was diagnosed with rheumatoid arthritis. There was no family history of the disease. Many relatives and close friends later felt that it was caused by all the tension he shouldered in his early years.

QRG tried allopathic medicine but the results were far from heartening. He then spent fifteen days in Patiala to take some Ayurvedic treatment. The pain in his joints would subside and then resurface with a vengeance. During these bouts, he would be bedridden for days together. But the moment the pain eased, QRG would return with a bang. Such was his willpower.

When rheumatoid arthritis strikes, most people begin to plan their retirement. Not QRG. In fact, his most stellar work in life came after 1975 when the illness was first detected.

By now, QRG had developed a taste for calculated risks. In 1981, he bought a computer for Rs 6 lakh. Havells was only the second company in Delhi to buy one. Then, in 1983, when the opportunity for inorganic expansion came, he was instantly interested.

Towers & Transformers, a sick electrical towers company, was up for sale. Its main attraction was the ten acres of land it owned in Sahibabad, located in Ghaziabad, very close to Delhi. Towers & Transformers was a part of the Premier Group, which also owned companies like Premier Cables and Premier Forgings. Hanuman Mal Periwal was the owner of this group and his office was in Connaught Place.

One of the dealers of Premier Cables was Guptajee & Co. Ramesh Sharda, who was the sales manager of Premier Cables, was QRG's friend. It was a recessionary time in 1983 and the Premier Group's financial health was not good. During one of their discussions, Sharda told QRG that Towers & Transformers could be up for sale since Periwal needed cash.

QRG found the prospect of owning ten acres near Delhi quite attractive. His main idea was to set up one large manufacturing unit, instead of the three small ones he had. QRG was introduced to Periwal at his residence in Hauz Khas. Contrary to what QRG had expected, Periwal seemed reluctant to sell as he too wanted to hold on to the real estate. He also had a sentimental reason for this—he had built a beautiful Hanuman temple on the site just a year ago and didn't want to let go of it.

Sharda and Periwal's chartered accountant, Manit Jaju, were able to convince him that cash at this juncture was more important than land—and the temple. QRG offered Rs 28 lakh to buy the unit. Surinderji and Surjitji resisted this investment because they felt that it was too big a risk for the group. But QRG was convinced and would not change his mind.

In the meantime, Periwal went to Singapore. By the time he came back, QRG had convinced his partners. However, now Periwal raised his price and asked for Rs 35 lakh. He had probably thought that QRG would not accept the price. But he didn't know that QRG was made of sterner stuff—he agreed to pay Rs 35 lakh and bought Towers & Transformers.

Jaju told me in March 2015 that the transaction went off smoothly. Once the deal was struck, he had advised his team to make the transition hassle free. In that meeting, Jaju also told me that he always found QRG different from the other traders in Bhagirath Palace. He looked like a long-term player and had the mindset of an industrialist rather than a trader.

The acquisition, worth Rs 35 lakh, was almost fully funded through bank loans. QRG's annual turnover at that time, between Havells and Guptajee & Co., was around Rs 3 crore, so the loan amounted to around 10 per cent of his annual revenues. This was a bold move especially since QRG did not have a clear plan for the factory he had just bought. Only later, when he saw the potential in electric meters did he use the Towers & Transformers land for it.

EIGHT

A Well-oiled Channel

This was also the time QRG started to build a national footprint. On a visit to the Central Power Research Institute in Bangalore for some meetings, he appointed a dealer in the city for Havells; Rakesh Mehrotra appointed dealers in Kanpur, while O.P. Gupta did the same in Calcutta.

The expansion was calibrated, which was the right way to go about it. Dealers are a part of your overall supply chain. Without an adequate manufacturing base, it is difficult to feed a large army of dealers.

Ever since Havells entered manufacturing in the 1970s, QRG maintained that one of his priorities was to target the trade, and establish comfortable, almost friendly relationships with his distributors and dealers. His foremost logic was that if the dealers were happy with you, they would aggressively push your products in the marketplace. This was against the grain—trade marketing was not considered important because it was a seller's market. Therefore, even before the concept of trade marketing became popular, Havells had absorbed, internalized and implemented this for almost two decades. It continues to be the prominent philosophy within the company. Every manager has imbibed it.

QRG's decision to focus on trade was driven by several factors. Since he had risen as a trader, he knew the mindset of a distributor or dealer quite well. Not only did he understand their apprehensions but he also appreciated what excited them.

From his business activities in the sixties, he learnt that respectable organizations always took care of their dealers. His personal experiences with Fort Gloster Industries reinforced this. When Shri Niwas Bangur insisted that QRG meet his father, Narsing Dass Bangur, this gesture showed the importance the company gave to its dealers and distributors.

Most importantly, QRG saw that if the trade was excited about a brand or product, sales went up. If the opposite was the case, sales suffered. He found that the difference between success and failure was the difference in aggression, passion and interest that the trade showed in a brand.

Companies that were arrogant or complacent about their dealers took a beating. They may have the best products, the best advertising and promotions, but their ability to push their products was limited because of the strained trade relationships.

Distributors and dealers were, therefore, always topmost on QRG's mind. Over the decades, despite the frenetic growth in the number of traders that Havells dealt with, he evolved various ways to keep in touch with them, listen to them, and glean market information from them.

He built personal, almost family-like, relationships with some of the big distributors and dealers, and this included his neighbours in Bhagirath Palace.

QRG used to notice how large companies such as Larsen & Toubro and English Electric would have dealer meets in five-star hotels. He too organized one in 1984—at the Taj Palace Hotel. Even though I was all of fifteen at that time, I went and negotiated the rates at the Tata-owned hotel in south Delhi. The event was hugely successful. And QRG had made an unambiguous statement in the market— dealers were of the utmost importance to him.

Havells began to organize regular offline hangouts with its distributors and dealers. All of them were invited for a social gathering every year where the atmosphere would be informal and friendly.

Dealers often came with their families, so these events were more like family holidays for both the company's managers and traders. Distributors and dealers openly interacted with QRG and discussed the market, their professional problems, as well as family grouses.

On many occasions, I would witness a particular dealer talk about the problems he had with his wife, children or close relatives. QRG would listen intently, and then advise him. He was truly interested and did not get involved just for the sake of it.

When quizzed about wasting his time over the dealers' personal problems, QRG told me that marketing, sales and trade are not about the management or business acumen of a person. A dealer may be exceptionally good at his work but unless he is free from nagging personal problems, it would be impossible for him to give his best.

While we were always thinking about how to improve dealer engagement, a chance meeting with Brijmohan Lall Munjal, who was then chairman of Hero MotoCorp (it was then known as Hero Honda), the country's largest maker of two-wheelers, helped us take it to the next level.

In June 2004, we had gone to Shimla on vacation and were staying at the Wildflower Hall. There, in the lobby, QRG saw the grand old man of the Indian motorcycle market. Not one to miss an opportunity, QRG walked up to him and introduced himself. Munjal was warm and said that he had heard of us, especially of the fact that we took good care of our dealers. He said we could look at dealer engagement together and agreed to meet us in Delhi.

QRG would say in his own unique way of imparting wisdom: *'Mullah sabak nahi dega, par ghar to aane dega.'* There are always good things to be learnt from big people.

Once we were back, QRG and I went to Munjal's office at Basant Lok in south Delhi. It is a cramped market, not the kind of place where one would expect to find the country's largest two-wheeler maker. Many people say that the Munjal family thinks the office has been lucky for them and therefore do not want to move out.

During the meeting, we realized how deeply Munjal was involved with his dealers when he asked us if the children of some of his dealers could engage in business with Havells. We also learnt how lavishly he spent on dealer meetings. We came back all charged up from the meeting. That very year, we took our dealers on their first overseas visit to Bangkok.

There was no turning back after that. In 2011, we took them to London where we booked the entire Grosvenor

House for them. On the last evening there, we organized a red-carpet event, something the hotel did only for celebrities. We went all out and this ensured that our relationship became a barrier for new players entering the sector. We started Galaxy Stores to sell Havells products especially for children of dealers who did not want to work at their parents' old shops. In 2015, we started the Young Entrepreneurs' Forum to understand these youngsters better.

When QRG was alive, during our daily morning meetings in the office, whenever the debate was about pricing, marketing strategy, product launch or market trends, he would invariably dial one of our distributors or dealers, or several of them, and ask questions about the topic on the speakerphone.

All of us would then hear what the trade had to say, or what it felt we should do. QRG would try to incorporate their views in our decisions. This happened in almost every meeting—we learnt ground realities from the trade and they felt important about their involvement in our internal affairs. This further strengthened our bond.

Traders would be delighted if their suggestions were implemented. This is something that QRG possibly learnt from Carnegie—an entrepreneur should make his stakeholders feel as if the company's decision was theirs.

This did not imply that QRG would implement everything the traders told him. Most often his decisions would be contrary to theirs. As I mentioned earlier, when the consensus among traders was that we should launch economy-priced fans, QRG had completely different thoughts. He formulated his marketing and sales strategy to sell high-quality, high-price products. At the end of the day, QRG had a mind of his own.

It is now an established norm within the company that every manager and division head also needs to think about the implications of any decision on the trade. Each one of us tries to replicate the emotional connection that QRG had with the dealers. For instance, a dealer from Bhatinda in Punjab, who had engaged in a Rs 10-crore deal with us, met QRG in Delhi. In an informal conversation, he told QRG, 'I do business with almost three dozen companies, but Havells is the only one with which I am emotionally attached.' I have heard similar endorsements from dozens of our distributors and dealers. The moral of the story is that a personal and passionate relationship with them is important.

In this respect, QRG showed the way to all of us. Between 1995 and 2000, I would regularly go to Bhagirath Palace with him and talk to the traders even though Havells had moved to our Civil Lines office in 1987. We would end up spending the entire day discussing everything from A to Z of the trends in the electrical goods business over lunch and endless cups of tea. It gave us valuable insights into the market that were better than any armchair research and analysis.

From 2000 onwards, as our trade network grew, regular phone conversations enabled us to stay in touch with the trade. In addition, every month or two, QRG would invite 100-odd dealers to his office and discuss market-related issues with them. He would call dozens of dealers home for lunch or dinner to make them feel like a part of his family. We would spend an entire day, either in Delhi or outside, and merely listen to the trade. Their doubts would be discussed and their feedback would be absorbed.

We thought that as we grew from a Rs 500-crore to a Rs 5000-crore (in annual turnover) company, we would find it increasingly difficult to maintain the same relationship with the trade. But I can say with justifiable pride and satisfaction, we have managed it. Every manager, whether at the headquarters or branch office, contributes towards maintaining this manufacturer–dealer connection.

In any industry in every country, the basic premise is that the business interests of the manufacturer and its dealers differ widely; they are two ends of a spectrum. But the success lies with the entrepreneur who can create a win-win situation for both. As QRG would say, 'I may be in a position to earn Rs 100 crore at the expense of the trade. But I would rather earn Rs 90 crore and leave the rest as goodwill with the dealers.'

NINE

Sibling Rivalry

While business boomed for Havells, QRG faced another personal turmoil. The second family fight erupted in the eighties. This time, Surinderji, his younger brother, who had joined the business, moved out. My father paid cash over a six-month period to buy Surinderji's share of the business.

A sort of unstated sibling rivalry had ensued between QRG and Surinderji. In fact, in 1975, before the Kirti Nagar factory came up, the younger brother shifted out of the joint residence at Civil Lines and took a house at Roop Nagar. In 1980 or 1981, he built a house at Kalyan Vihar and moved there.

No one thought much about it, and most people blamed it on the usual bickering in any Indian family, this time between Surinderji's wife and the other women in the household, including my mother. Still, the two families remained close, and would meet regularly at important festivals and other social events.

Within seven years, by 1982, Surinderji's complaints had turned into loud grumbles. He disagreed with my father's decision to set up new factories in quick succession; he felt that they should instead build up the group's cash reserves to ward off future crises.

Surinderji thought that QRG was a rash risk-taker who could ruin the business one day and take it to the cleaners. He believed that one wrong financial decision would wipe Havells and Guptajee & Co. off the map. Matters came to a head in 1983. Against the wishes of his younger brother, my father went ahead and acquired Towers & Transformers, a seemingly risky deal.

Surinderji openly revolted; this was unacceptable to him. He believed that my father had no idea how to run the business—he had spent Rs 35 lakh, most of it through bank loans, for a dud factory whose only asset was the ten-acre plot in distant Sahibabad, where the demand for real estate was almost non-existent within Delhi's business community. He was plagued with questions—what would he do with the land? How would he repay the loan? What will happen to the group's cash reserves? Surinderji thought QRG had lost the plot.

It was a classic clash between brothers in business. Invariably, the elder one, or the one who takes critical business decisions, is both confident and ambitious. He is sure he is on the right track. He enters the areas that are unthinkable for the other. He sets the future agenda.

Mostly, the younger ones, or those who are usually prepared to take a back seat for the moment, are horrified at the other sibling's risk appetite. They feel duty-bound to stop him at any cost.

Sibling rivalry in the first generation of business families can result from other insecurities too. Normally, of all the brothers and sisters (rare in India) who are involved in the business, one leads the pack. Therefore, when the second generation comes of age, the patriarch, or the leader among the first-generation members, has this inherent desire to preserve the empire for his children, rather than for his nephews and nieces. He wants to keep the businesses within his immediate family.

If they remain unresolved or linger on, such intra-generational struggles are enough to destroy the majority of business families in the first generation, and most of the remaining ones in the second. If the family survives into the third generation, similar differences invariably break out between the younger members.

By the third generation, the number of members multiplies rapidly. Apart from the patriarch's sons, there may be cousins and other relatives, who are somewhat active in the business, or at least have a stake in it. It may be that they cannot get along with many of the others or that their ambitions differ.

That apart, the size of the business expands so much that each member is confident enough to demand his or her share. By this time, ego, jealousy, greed and power together create centrifugal forces beyond anyone's control. This creates ruptures in the family.

Sibling splits can either be negotiated peacefully or through force. For amicable solutions to be reached, magnanimity and large-heartedness are critical factors. They tend to be rare when the brothers, sisters and cousins in each generation sit across the table, if they do sit together. In fact, in the first and third generation, such instances tend to be rarer.

Negotiations are tough in the third generation because of the sheer number of members. In the first, the difficulties arise because whichever brother/sister retains the fledgling business, and it is generally too small to divide, has to part with enough cash to satisfy the other siblings. The latter has to feel that they got a good deal.

Fortunately, although it was not a case of sibling rivalry, this is what QRG did with his uncle, P.C. Gupta, after he paid him Rs 45,000 that was negotiated through an open informal auction.

Through 1982 and 1983, Surinderji demanded a separation. He took the matter to O.P. Gupta in Calcutta on several occasions but he managed to pacify him. In 1984, he once again demanded that he be allowed to part ways. I remember QRG and my mother going to his place and somehow managing to convince him to stay yet again.

Two months later, when O.P. Gupta was in Delhi, some sort of a pact was made whereby QRG would not undertake any further expansion. Surinderji's wish to conserve cash was granted. This could not have been to QRG's liking because he took calculated risks and dreamt big. But I guess he made this sacrifice in order to keep the family together. It was an uneasy peace.

It so happened that soon QRG undertook some repairs at one of the factories. Surinderji, who mistook it as construction for a fresh investment, exploded in anger and complained to O.P. Gupta. A split was now imminent. Both the brothers went to Calcutta to present their case to O.P. Gupta. Then it was decided that they should go their separate ways.

To sort out the second family separation, O.P. Gupta flew down once again to Delhi. Yet again, all the three stakeholders—QRG, Surinderji and O.P. Gupta—sat in my father's house over glasses of lassi. Yet again, my father agreed to his business partner's cash demands. The split was sealed.

At that time, Havells was valued at Rs 1 crore. Since Surinderji owned 27 per cent of the company, he demanded Rs 27 lakh. The offer was that he would be paid Rs 20 lakh in cash and would be given two plots of land Havells had bought, in Okhla and Burari, which were estimated to be worth Rs 7 lakh. Initially, Surinderji agreed. Later, he demanded the entire amount in cash. QRG agreed to pay him Rs 27 lakh over a period of six months; and he kept his promise.

Money was not an issue by then. The revenue of the company grew steadily to Rs 4 crore by the early eighties. After this rupture, my father was now totally in control of the business. Surjitji, QRG's brother-in-law, who was also a partner in the business, was a fierce loyalist. Since he had a technical bent of mind, QRG gave him responsibilities that matched his temperament. He had great respect for QRG and continued to believe in the Havells story.

In the split, QRG gave away a shell company he had set up, Allied Agencies, to Surinderji. With the money he had got, Surinderji opened Allied Agencies at Bhagirath Palace to deal in electrical goods. After a few years, he started making switchgear under the SHI brand.

Surinderji's departure did not affect the business much. It was a personal loss for QRG no doubt, but he did not let it derail his life. The relationship between QRG and

Surinderji remained lukewarm. After 2000, there was an improvement, but the earlier warmth was gone.

From my early days, I remember QRG being very busy all the time. That's because he was very passionate about work. In the morning, he used to go and meet officers of various government departments for the cable business. Later, he would use the time to call his dealers at distant places. I remember when direct dialling (STD) started, he would ask us to dial his associates on the rotor phone. It would often take us twenty attempts to get through to one number.

He used to work the whole day at Guptajee & Co. and Havells, and would get home by 7.30 p.m., having left home at 9 a.m.

The whole family would have dinner together, including my grandfather, Lachhman Das, who passed away in 1996. At the dining table, QRG would not ramble about the daily grind or business. Instead, he would talk of values and traditions. We would also discuss current affairs. Everybody was encouraged to speak freely. It was something we all looked forward to.

Outwardly, he wouldn't show too much affection towards the three of us. He was stern but would seldom get angry. But if we ever told a lie, he would get very upset.

We did not get any pocket money when we were young, which we frequently complained about, especially because most other students would come to school with coins jingling in their pockets. But we were always given whatever we needed. Later, we started to get pocket money but the amount was limited. QRG and my mother wanted to inculcate in us respect for hard-earned money.

Our habits were modest. We would get ice cream once a week or once in two weeks. All our vacations were impromptu and we would frequently end up at hill stations like Shimla and Nainital. The hotels were pretty ordinary. It was only in the eighties that we started staying at good properties.

In the summer of 1978, we had planned a long vacation of eight or nine days in Bombay. The night before we were to leave, Shri Niwas Bangur called QRG and told him that a big order for cables from DESU was at a crucial stage and he should therefore stay put in Delhi. QRG was strongly entrenched at DESU; so, we were told to unpack, and were promised a visit to Bombay the following year. In return, we got to see a film every week during the holidays. Those were innocent times—postponement of pleasure, unlike now, was looked upon as a virtue.

As a child, I remember that money was never a problem in the family. Life was comfortable but not extravagant. When we went to restaurants, we would look at the prices on menu cards; we would also decide to eat dessert elsewhere to save some money.

In 1985, QRG started occasionally taking us to the more expensive five-star hotels so that we understood the etiquette of a fancy place. He wanted us to imbibe the nuances—what to order, how to eat with fork and knife, etc.

Much later in life, my school friends would confide that they never thought I was the son of a successful businessman. My first holiday abroad with the family was after I had joined college in the US; my parents had come over from Delhi and we had gone for sightseeing. But I had travelled abroad earlier on school trips. One such trip was to Singapore with Ajesh.

My father often said, 'Life is a mystery. It is difficult, if not impossible, to unravel and understand. So, one needs to always have one's feet on the ground.'

In spite of his busy schedule, QRG would take time out for his few indulgences—cricket being one of them. We used to go to watch Test matches at Delhi's Feroz Shah Kotla stadium. Seats were booked and the extended family would gather to enjoy the game. I remember watching several cricket matches with him. Many crucial games, like the historic 1983 World Cup final, when India defeated the mighty West Indies, we watched together on television.

Despite coming from a modest background, QRG was a man of good taste. He bought furniture from New Age, the best store in Delhi, even in the seventies. In Delhi, QRG would take us to good restaurants like Woodlands, Host and Gaylord.

And all three of us—Ajesh, Geeta and I—were good at studies. This was important to QRG. He never had the time to teach us but always kept a close watch on our academic performance. When Ajesh got 98 per cent in his Class XII exams, QRG was over the moon. I remember there was a family get-together in those days, and QRG proudly told everybody present about his elder son's achievement. Nothing can hide the pride and happiness of a very communicative man.

Immediately after he had cleared the Class XII exams in 1983, Ajesh got admission in two of the most prestigious engineering colleges in the country—the Indian Institute of Technology Kanpur and Delhi College of Engineering. The first, of course, was at the top of the pecking order but QRG and our mother insisted he join Delhi College of Engineering. What may have played on QRG's mind was his ill health—he didn't want to be separated from his son.

After passing out of Delhi College of Engineering in 1987, Ajesh joined Havells. It was a lateral entry. He was the heir apparent from day one, and he knew it.

As far as studies were concerned, I was following in the able footsteps of Ajesh. I was always among the top two or three in the class. After studying till class XII at St Xavier's, I took admission in the Shri Ram College of Commerce, the highly respected and sought-after institution of higher learning in Delhi.

Geeta was my senior at Shri Ram College of Commerce by three years. My parents had begun to look around for a suitable boy for her. She married Manish Agarwal in 1986 while in the third year of college. Her in-laws too lived in Civil Lines and were in the construction business. Their firm was called Clarion Builders, which was later renamed Satya Developers.

Geeta's marriage in 1986 was an announcement to the trade that QRG was a cut above the rest. The money spent and the class of the wedding was among the best in Delhi in those times. True to his style of delegation, QRG gave the entire responsibility for the bandobast to his friend, Bhim Sain Gupta, the owner of Plaza Cables. He sold off an extra shop in Bhagirath Palace, Geeta International, for Rs 22 lakh and used the proceeds to pay for the grand wedding celebrations. Shri Niwas Bangur also attended the wedding.

Meanwhile, the pundit who had played matchmaker for Geeta also found a bride for Ajesh, who tied the knot the following year.

TEN

<hr>

Shah Bina Pat Nahi

The first signs of a change in the country's economic outlook had started to emerge. Indira Gandhi had swept back to power in 1980 after being booted out in 1977; wrecked by internal strife, the makeshift Janata Party experiment had failed within two years.

Backed by a stable government, Indira Gandhi allowed the first whiff of liberalization to float into the country's business environment. During the early eighties, Pranab Mukherjee, the then Union finance minister, attempted to partly unleash the country's latent entrepreneurial spirits through his pro-reform budgets.

Among the several measures that he initiated in his three budgets in the early eighties, Mukherjee reduced the interest rates for the corporate sector, encouraged investments from NRIs, rationalized the tax structure, and encouraged savings.

A caveat is in order here. Compared to the policies initiated by P.V. Narasimha Rao and Manmohan Singh in 1991, Indira Gandhi and Pranab Mukherjee's reforms of the 1980s seem insignificant. But juxtaposed against

Jawaharlal Nehru's economic policies of the fifties, the changes initiated in the eighties signified a quantum leap.

And when Rajiv Gandhi became the prime minister in 1984, there were definite moves towards a more open economy, though full liberalization of economic policy would have to wait for a few more years. This is the time that Japanese two-wheeler makers like Honda, Yamaha and Suzuki first came to India. A mistrust of multinational corporations—a hangover of our colonial and socialist past—started to melt away.

QRG read the tea leaves well. He saw the window of opportunity to acquire technology. Developing these technologies in-house would have consumed a lot of our time and resources, and there was no guarantee of success. A convenient way out was to get into an agreement with an overseas company that already had the technology. There was no wisdom in reinventing the wheel.

To scout for partners abroad in key product categories, QRG appointed Ajesh. QRG encouraged him to attend trade fairs at Hanover and other places to identify potential partners. This initial contact would be followed by visits to each other's factories. It would take five to six months to wrap up these agreements.

Many of these companies were interested in India, a burgeoning virgin market. Most of them were impressed with our dealer network. Forming these partnerships was quite an achievement—not everybody had the wherewithal to do it.

In 1987, we signed our first collaboration for miniature circuit breakers, or MCBs, with Geyer of Germany. It developed into a strong alliance. QRG had a close personal relationship with its promoter, Albert Geyer. So much so, Geyer bought a 12 per cent stake in Havells when we made our initial public offer in 1993. He was a tall and friendly man. Whenever we travelled to Germany, he would invite us home to dinner. His children would show us around. And when they came to India, we would try to reciprocate the hospitality.

Unfortunately, in the late nineties, Geyer was diagnosed with cancer. After he died in 1999, it was up to his daughter, Sabine, who worked in the finance department, to run the company. His brothers had retired from work and his son wasn't interested in the business. The company, which had been hugely successful in the nineties, especially after the German reunification, went into decline.

There came a stage when Sabine offered to sell the company to us. We were interested in one unit in Greece which made the MCBs but the talks did not reach any conclusion. Then, in 2004, Sabine said that she would like to sell the stake in Havells to raise cash. That is when we bought back the 12 per cent stake that the Geyer family had purchased.

In 2005–06, she finally sold off the company. After that, our contact became sporadic—it was restricted to short email exchanges once a year or so.

After Geyer, there were two more technical collaborations—Peterreins for changeover switches and Schiele for residual current circuit breakers, or RCCBs. Both were German companies. We paid them some money upfront at the time of signing the collaboration, and a certain percentage of the sales as royalty.

Around that time, QRG also decided to give Havells a national footprint. His first destination for a branch outside Delhi was Calcutta. Perhaps because of his closeness to O.P. Gupta, he felt the latter could keep an eye on it. By 1985, his son, Yogesh Kumar Gupta, who we all call Vickyji, had joined the business.

QRG asked Vickyji to look for a suitable place for the office in Calcutta. He identified two spaces, both in and around Park Street. The first was cheaper but its entrance was cramped and shabby. QRG chose the other one. The office was the face of the company and QRG did not want to leave customers with a bad first impression.

This was his lifelong philosophy. Looks and presentation were equally important for him. He took care in the way he dressed—old photographs show him dressed smartly in dark trousers, a light shirt and a thin black tie.

QRG had minimal educational background. He was not really aware of management jargon like JIT (just in time, the Japanese system of keeping inventory stock at the shop floor to the minimum), inventory management and finance transformation. But he instinctively imbibed the combined philosophies into his business.

In the early nineties, when I joined the business, QRG gave a very high, and sometimes the highest, priority to finance and the CFO. *'Guru bina gat nahin, Shah bina pat nahi,'* he was fond of saying. Just like you need a teacher in life, you need complete backing of investors and lenders. He also believed that every successful business person needs somebody smart to handle the finances. He regularly mentioned that the CFO was critical to the success of the business—he had to be involved in all the strategic and tactical decisions.

This is the reason why Rajesh Gupta, who joined us as an accountant in 1979, and rose to become the CFO and executive director in 1993, would always be present during the morning meetings that QRG held daily with his senior managers. Rajesh's inputs were taken seriously and, in many ways, he was responsible for what Havells would become one day. He has been a critical pillar in our growth story.

Rajesh worked closely with QRG. He was in tune with QRG's mind, and anticipated his thought processes. He was always ready even if our plans seemed a bit risky and rash. In most companies, the CFO is the conscience keeper, holding back and asking if the balance sheet could support certain expansions. The CFO in Havells played a much larger role. He questioned if our expansion plans were tenable but also worked hard to financially translate the vision and strategies of the management into reality.

'According to me, the function of the finance department is to be friendly with the production and marketing divisions. We are there to support them, as also the allied stakeholders like the sales team, our distributors and dealers. We never wanted to make the Havells juggernaut stop, stall or slow down. We want it to grow steadily, and do everything to achieve those objectives,' Rajesh says about his role in the company.

In fact, from the late seventies, QRG's finance team innovated and created products that formed the pillars to support the success of Havells.

Cash flows on a daily basis and requirement of working capital are two of the most important reasons why companies go bust at any stage of their life cycles. This can happen early on, when cash mismanagement can kill companies at birth. This is why most small businesses die an untimely death early on in their lives.

Even when a company has been in existence for decades and grown to the size of a behemoth, cash problems can decimate it. Aggressive expansions, ambitious investments, and an inability to control the resultant shocks in cash management and planning have wreaked havoc on several businesses.

This was not to be with Havells because of QRG's belief in the CFO and the finance department, and his decision to make the CFO participate in, sometimes shape, and often drive growth. Many of the successful take-off points in our history were driven by the CFO.

During the eighties, we faced finance-related problems typical of any young company. Such issues generally arise from three factors—the transition-related financial complexities; relationships with lenders, especially banks; and tensions, mostly linked to payments, with suppliers and buyers.

Trading has a comfortable finance cycle—the trick lies in the number of times you can rotate the cash in a monthly or quarterly cycle. It is management of how much you can afford to buy, what kind of credit period you can give to the sellers, and how soon you can recover the money from the buyers. Since there is no value addition in between, there are no additional risks.

Manufacturing is a more complex structure. Suddenly, the number of suppliers and buyers grows. At the same time, inventory management of raw materials and final products becomes critical. In addition, there are finance-related problems with labour and expansion.

Investments of any form, in higher production or new products, influence cash management processes. You invest immediately but the returns take time to materialize. In addition, you need to arrange finances externally since the business itself may not be able to generate the requisite funds. So, one has to think of interest and loan payments.

When you are a trader, there are generally five or six suppliers catering to double the number of buyers. In manufacturing, the combined figure can increase manifold. The payment schedules are scattered, and someone has to be paid every week or daily. So, payments become a thorny issue. Labour has to be paid regularly because any break in the continuity of production can cause unmanageable losses. Each time a payment goes haywire, suppliers queue up outside the office.

Most importantly, the manufacturing business is rooted in external finance, mostly from lenders like banks. Every company needs additional capital to improve cash flows and manage the working capital requirements. Even if the company has the option to raise money from the stock markets, or any other stock arrangement (angel investors, venture capitalists and private equity), it has to manage the expectations of the investors, which is quite different from traditional lenders.

Since we went public only in the early nineties, we depended on bank finance to manage our business before that. Therefore, our relationship with the bankers were important. The banking environment in the eighties in

India was quite different from what it is today. Now, small and medium businesses have access to loans through several incentivized schemes. Back then, banks avoided such businesses because of the inherent risks. They lent either if they knew the promoters, or if the latter had the right 'connections'.

From the beginning, QRG was aware of these complexities. He may not have been trained in finance but he knew its importance in the manufacturing scheme of things. He realized that the wheel of production moved smoothly if the grease of cordial relationships with suppliers, distributors, dealers and bankers was applied.

Therefore, in the eighties, he did everything to put the finances in order, and not let any crisis related to vendors and bankers impact Havells. He also took the necessary financial risks to expand the business, even if it meant battling internally with senior managers, including his family.

In the early 1980s, as mentioned earlier, QRG made the first big investment gambit when he took over the sick Towers & Transformers plant, even when he did not wish to manufacture the latter's product, because of the potential he saw in the excess land owned by the company.

Over months and years, it led to some form of a financial squeeze as we set up another unit there, which added to the revenues and profits after some time. In addition, the takeover led to internal criticism, especially from QRG's brother and partner, Surinderji, who separated from the business for this reason. Most important, the acquisition led to jittery suppliers, whose payments were delayed due to the investment in Towers & Transformers. Many of the raw material suppliers thought that they needed to avoid Havells.

QRG immediately jumped into the fray before the suppliers took drastic action. He called them and said that they had two options—take immediate payments with no guarantee of a future relationship, or wait for the payment cycle, which would soon stabilize and continue the business relationship. The vendors wanted to use the threat to put pressure on Havells but after hearing this, they retreated immediately. It saved Havells from its manufacturing-linked financial problem.

In retrospect, I often think about QRG's motives and thought process. Was it sheer bluster because there was no way the company could have repaid the creditors if they wanted immediate cash? Was it foresight since he understood the need of the vendors to continue a long-term relationship with Havells? Was it part luck, part strategy to tackle the suppliers? It was perhaps a combination of all the three factors.

Over the years, I found that other businessmen often faced a similar situation. Most shared that they usually played the same game without knowing the end result. With their backs to the wall, they had to use similar threats against the creditors. It was a question of who blinked first and, fortunately, in this case, the suppliers did.

Knowing QRG, however, I think it was a part of his strategy. It was his inherent desire to be honest and transparent with the stakeholders, whoever they might be and whatever the financial state of his companies might be. He adopted the same approach when he dealt with bankers in those days.

During the late eighties, he negotiated with lenders thrice to get Havells out of trouble. One of the most important occasions was when he had to sort out problems related to recovery of dues from the state electricity boards (SEBs) that had purchased our electricity meters.

Getting money out of any government department or agency was as difficult in those days as it is today. Bureaucratic hurdles, chaotic financial planning, plus dependence on government's support, which never arrived on time, delayed payment by months, and sometimes even years. For a small business like ours—the turnover ranged between Rs 2 crore and Rs 15 crore in the eighties—even if a few tens of thousands of rupees stuck somewhere could stretch our meagre finances.

In the case of the SEBs, the problems were compounded because of the manner in which they received money to buy their equipment. The Central government funded financial institutions in the power sector, like Power Finance Corporation (PFC) and Rural Electrification Corporation (REC). The PFC and REC, in turn, refinanced the electricity boards to fund the latter's purchases. It was only then that the money came to vendors like us if the SEBs were efficient enough to write the cheques.

When there were delays at the SEB, our suppliers wouldn't get paid on time. In those days, as a child, I remember seeing some supplier or the other waiting for his payment in the office. The vendors would queue up outside the finance department every day and wait—sometimes patiently and sometimes angrily. The CFO would end up spending half of each day dealing with creditors in a bid to cajole and calm them down.

I remember Rajesh would often complain about this headache, which never seemed to go away. Payments were always stuck at some SEB or the other.

QRG realized that this had to stop if Havells were to focus on the actual business of funding growth. He said we had to find a solution with the banks in terms of higher working capital limits, even if it meant we had to spend more on interest and loan repayments. But it was worth our while for several reasons—the suppliers' queues would vanish and our image and credibility among them would rise. And we could seriously pursue business strategies. More importantly, the extra interest we paid to the banks would be adjusted against the interest we paid for late payments.

However, when we met the bankers, they flatly refused our proposal. They said that we had exhausted our borrowing limits (based on the formula, working capital equals value of stocks + debtors—money owed to creditors). They added that our credit cycle (or the money owed to creditors in terms of the value of daily production) was too high at seventy days, when the average for a business our size was thirty to thirty-five days.

To find a solution to this vexing problem, QRG told the banks that we did not need additional working capital. But could they do us a favour? We would give them the list of our suppliers, the amount owed to them, and the payment schedules. Could they pay directly to the suppliers within thirty to thirty-five days, and give us additional time to repay the banks? They agreed, and instantly our creditors' period came tumbling down from seventy to thirty to thirty-five days!

QRG dealt in a transparent fashion with the banks on two other critical occasions in those days. The first was when our factory in Kirti Nagar, the first one we set up, was razed to the ground in a fire in 1990. Everything turned to ashes. When he came back home at 4 a.m., QRG was depressed. My mother asked him a very pertinent question—did anyone lose their life in the fire? When QRG said that there were no casualties, she asked him to rest, reminding him that material things could be replaced.

However, this was easier said than done. QRG wanted the banks to give us another Rs 10–20 lakh to rebuild the plant and commence operations. Only when he openly told them what had happened and shared his plans to increase revenues from the same factory, did they see his earnestness and sanctioned new loans. Bankers need to trust their clients, and they had absolute faith in QRG.

During another instance, when we wanted a further increase in the working capital limits, Rajesh's predecessor failed miserably. That's when QRG appointed Rajesh as the new CFO, and urged him to deal with the banks. To his dismay, Rajesh found that the banks were unhappy because Havells had not submitted the requisite financial documents and information to the lenders for months.

'When I told them I would definitely do so in the next few weeks, they said they would only consider the proposal for a loan increase after they got the documents. After my discussion with QRG, I spent fifteen to twenty hours a day that weekend getting all the paperwork in order. On Monday, I went to the bankers with a complete set of documents, which comprised more than 1000 pages. They saw our earnestness and sanctioned a higher loan limit the same day,' Rajesh said.

ELEVEN

Change of Guard

I returned from the United States after completing my studies in May 1992. By then India had taken definitive steps towards becoming an open economy. Private enterprise was no longer a dirty word. A whole new world of possibilities had opened up for businessmen. A handful of top-notch businessmen had got together to demand protection from multinational corporations, under the aegis of the Bombay Club, but that couldn't stem the tide of liberalization.

Ajesh was well set in Havells, so QRG perhaps brought me in with lesser enthusiasm. I spent a lot of my initial days at the Kirti Nagar factory, where I learnt how to control inventory and improve productivity. I was able to implement some of the business lessons I had learnt at Wake Forest University, North Carolina.

In September 1992, I joined the Havells board. Ajesh was already a part of it and he was firmly in control. All the foreigners who came would negotiate with him. To create a niche for myself, I started shadowing our marketing in-charge, Krishan Lal Malik. Before Havells, he had worked with big corporations such as Siemens and Standard

Electricals. At fifty-five, he had enough experience and a mind of his own. That I was the owner's son didn't impress him one bit, even as I followed him all over India.

I was squeezed between two strong personalities, Ajesh and Malik, which did no good to my confidence. I married Sangeeta in 1993. She had done her BCom (honours) from the prestigious Lady Shri Ram College of Delhi. She came from a family of garment exporters—their firm was called Nath Brothers. Since she hailed from a business family, she adjusted very well into our household. Apart from the new-found marital bliss, little changed in life for me— QRG continued to repose his faith in Ajesh.

A year after I had joined the business, QRG decided it was time to get Havells listed on the stock market. At that time, many private companies were looking to get listed. Indo-Asian Fusegear, a company formed in 1990 after the promoters of Standard Electricals decided to part ways, had got listed in 1992—its public issue was oversubscribed forty times. Several others had also managed to raise large sums of money from the market.

This led to the desire to get Havells listed as well. We had bought a piece of land at Faridabad to make contactors that are used in power control panels. The project cost was Rs 4 crore. The public issue was meant to raise funds for that investment.

Our internal calculations indicated that we should issue the shares, which had a face value of Rs 10, at a premium of Rs 15 per share. Since we wanted to do business only with the best, we decided to hand over the mandate to SBI Caps, the country's topmost merchant banker of the time but its Mumbai head office refused to entertain us. The

L–R: Geeta (sister), the author, QRG, Vinod (mother), Ajesh (brother) in 1978

Standing (L–R): P.C. Gupta, G.R. Gupta, L.R. Gupta, Sarwa Mal
(QRG's grandfather), L.D. Gupta (QRG's father), O.P. Gupta;
sitting (L–R): P.C. Gupta's wife, G.R. Gupta's wife, L.R. Gupta's wife, QRG's aunts,
Sheelaji and Sitaji, L.D. Gupta's wife (QRG's mother), O.P. Gupta's wife, circa 1955

PUBLIC HIGH SCHOOL, BANUR (PEPSU)
X CLASS (1953-54).

QRG (sitting second from right) during his teaching days in 1953–54

L–R: O.P. Gupta, L.D. Gupta (QRG's father), G.R. Gupta, Surinder (QRG's brother), P.C. Gupta, D.P. Gupta (L.R. Gupta's son), K.K. Gupta (QRG's brother), V.P. Gupta (G.R. Gupta's son), QRG, circa 1970

QRG outside Havells Office, Bhagirath Palace, in 1971

On winning the election as president of DETA in 1973–74

A jubilant QRG with friends after winning DETA elections in 1973–74

Havan ceremony at the Kirti Nagar plant in 1976

Tea session with President Giani Zail Singh
L–R: Geeta, President Zail Singh, Manish Agarwal (Geeta's husband),
L.D. Gupta (QRG's father), QRG, Vinod, the author in 1986

QRG receiving the Udyog Ratna Award from
President Shankar Dayal Sharma in 1987

QRG shaking hands with Albert Geyer at the joint-venture meet in 1993

QRG at the signing of a joint-venture agreement with Dorman Smith in 1996

QRG at the acquisition of Standard Electricals in 2000

Standing (L–R): Rajesh Gupta, the author, Ameet Gupta; sitting (L–R): Surjit Gupta, QRG in 2003

QRG receiving the Distinguished Entrepreneurship Award from
the PHD Chamber of Commerce and Industry in 2004

Baba Ramdev inaugurating QRG Towers, Noida, in 2008

QRG at an all-India sales conference in Grosvenor House, London, UK, in 2011

Day out with family: The author with QRG, mother, wife, Sangeeta, and children, Abhinav and Aradhana, in 2011

QRG at the signing of the joint-venture deal with Yaming Lighting in 2011

Azim Premji with QRG and the author in 2013

QRG receiving the E&Y Entrepreneur Award in 2013

QRG at a breakfast meeting with the Sylvania team in 2013

merchant banker felt that Havells could not charge any premium, given the stock market environment.

The stock market was in a slump after the Harshad Mehta scam in 1992. The buzz of 1990 had started waning. The merchant banker felt that investors would be unwilling to pay a premium for Havells, and did not wish to be associated with a failed issue. We then approached SBI Caps' Delhi office with our calculations and numbers. They too refused to budge from the decision taken by the Mumbai office.

We were in a quandary. We knew we deserved a premium. And we did not want to delay the public issue. So, QRG decided to try a different tack. We met all our business partners, including distributors and dealers. We explained the reasons behind the issue, why we felt that our shares should be allotted at a premium, and how Rs 15 was justified based on the numbers.

Surprisingly, we saw huge enthusiasm among the dealers to buy the shares. They were willing to pay the premium, and excitedly wrote cheques. In no time, we realized that our issue was subscribed! We now met SBI Caps with the new information.

Once the merchant banker realized that there was no reason for the issue to fail even if the shares were sold at a premium, it agreed. In October 1993, the market revived a little and we hit it with our Rs 5-crore issue. The shares were sold at Rs 25 each (Rs 10 face value + Rs 15 premium), and the issue was oversubscribed four and a half times!

Once Havells was listed, its stock did not perform too well. It was clear that we had overprojected our business.

When performance fell short, investors were disillusioned and they dumped our stock. The company had started losing investor attention and the fact that Havells was Delhi-based (instead of Mumbai) also contributed to it. Many advised us to 'play the market', which was the norm at the time, but QRG would have none of it.

As the share price languished, QRG felt disillusioned and considered delisting the share. However, Rajesh insisted that the Havells scrip should continue to be traded on the exchange. His reasons were several—one, a listed firm is known among a larger set of investors, which would be an advantage if additional capital was required in the future. Two, being listed took care of growth and expansion in an indirect manner. The pressure on such firms to show better performance every quarter keeps the management consistently on its toes. It forces the promoters to seriously explore growth avenues. Finally, the quarter-to-quarter approach makes the management more accountable to its shareholders and, hence, to all the stakeholders.

QRG saw the logic and backtracked.

His frail health notwithstanding, QRG was satisfied with how his life was progressing. He had the personal and professional support of his two sons and the company was doing well.

QRG had planned to buy a larger house. To this end, he had bought another house, the ownership of which was disputed, in the same housing complex where we were living. His idea was to build a house each for his two sons. QRG managed to sort out the dispute and built another house at the second site. In 1993, he came across the opportunity to buy a 1700-square-yard plot, also in Civil

Lines. He realized that this suited his needs for a bigger house and clinched the deal overnight.

But ominous clouds were lurking on the horizon.

In the initial years, Ajesh, my older brother, had a great working relationship with QRG. Ajesh was an engineering graduate, and his skills and knowledge complemented QRG's natural wisdom and experience. Having passed out of the Delhi College of Engineering, he added the much-required technical edge to the business.

In the post-Surinderji split period, between 1985 and 1995, Ajesh contributed immensely to Havells's growth and helped translate QRG's new dreams into reality, most important of which were the three technical collaborations with German companies.

The workaholic and perfectionist that he was, Ajesh was the mastermind behind these agreements. He travelled abroad, and spoke to senior managers in MNCs to finalize critical contracts. He became a director in no time. Even at the time of our public issue, Ajesh did roadshows and addressed investors and media, though Rajesh and I were involved in the preparations for the IPO. He had charisma. And QRG had the perfect successor in Ajesh.

Unfortunately, in a few short years, the bonhomie turned sour.

Several factors were responsible for the rifts between QRG and Ajesh in the early nineties. The first was the difference in their management styles. Both were strong personalities and were endowed with immense self-belief and conviction.

QRG could, and did, take the final decisions. But he sought the opinions of all the stakeholders—from within the company and outside. He cut across hierarchies to obtain various viewpoints. Ajesh was more independent. Both approaches can yield results, but they cannot coexist in the same company. Since decisions have to be taken by a leader, he has to bear the responsibility. While Ajesh's was a top-down style, QRG's was a combination of flat and top-down.

Dual centres of power in corporate environments, which are different from each other, create a whole new set of problems. Loyalties among employees get divided. Since Ajesh was the heir apparent, and everyone including me knew it, many managers sided with him.

It would be wrong to blame Ajesh. This sort of rift is not uncommon in most workplaces; in fact, many owners/ CEOs/promoters encourage such divisions at the senior managers' levels.

QRG felt this approach would not work for Havells. He always wanted a transparent and politics-free organization.

The third factor that may have distanced Ajesh from QRG was family politics. In every family, there are some relatives, young and old, who try to influence some members. This is especially true in wealthy business families. It is a part of human nature, and one cannot do much about it.

The cumulative effect of the above factors was that it resulted in differences between father and son. In the beginning, such discussions happened at the dinner table, or over breakfast.

As in any other family, the ice would break over some pretext, and life would go on. Peace would reign until it was time for another debate on some other business-related issue.

In 1994, there was a disagreement between the two in the office. As a result, communication between them broke down. My brother felt that he was in the right, and the stand-off continued.

QRG thought this was just another incident and his elder son would come around, as he had done in the past. Sadly, this time the relationship was damaged beyond repair. In January 1995, Ajesh demanded separation.

Once again, QRG discussed this with his mentor, the Calcutta-based uncle, O.P. Gupta, who then chatted with Ajesh in Calcutta about various issues and finally convinced him to continue to work with his father. Things were quiet on the family front for a short time.

Then another disagreement erupted and this time Ajesh was adamant. He wanted to branch out on his own.

O.P. Gupta flew in to Delhi, with Vickyji, his youngest son, to settle matters between QRG and Ajesh. QRG chose O.P. Gupta because he felt his uncle was a balanced man and would therefore not short-change Ajesh. The family amicably reached a solution. It was acceptable to both QRG and Ajesh. QRG agreed to give his elder son a profitable factory—the one at Tilak Nagar. This factory used to produce meters under the Elymer Havells brand. Along with the factory, QRG ceded the Elymer brand to Ajesh.

Of the group's turnover of Rs 100 crore in 1995, 30 to 40 per cent was contributed by the electric meters unit in Tilak Nagar and also a similar percentage of the profits. QRG was unperturbed; his only concern was that Ajesh should be happy.

Privately, my parents were heartbroken. Not only because this had split the business empire, but also because the elder son was no longer in the same business or in the same house. Two years before, in 1993, the family had moved to a bigger house. We all thought we would live like one happy joint family thereafter, but that was not to be.

For QRG, it was a dual loss—of his elder son and business successor. For my mother, as is the case with most mothers, the elder son was the apple of her eye.

QRG once admitted: 'I was shattered; it was a big jolt to me. I never thought he would actually separate.'

But when it happened, it was again done amicably.

As he would often remind me, 'On the path to any kind of success, one has to make personal and other sacrifices. For me, the terms of the split were not about factories, revenues and profits, and what share who got. It was about being away from my eldest son. What he took in terms of profits did not matter, for he took away a part of my heart and soul with him. But it had to be done for sustenance.'

Successful people have a pattern in the manner in which they deal with personal crises. Almost all of them immerse themselves more into their business and profession. They work that much harder, they spend more hours at the office, and they force their mind to think only about work.

This was the first fortunate consequence of the 1995 split. QRG decided to focus only on business, and set ambitious growth targets. He said he wanted Havells to become a 300-crore-rupee company (in terms of turnover) in five years, an increase of five times from what he was left with. We did achieve this, and it roused passion, excitement and energy in our employees, especially among the senior managers.

Second, it helped me grow within the organization and emerge as a serious manager. While Ajesh was around, I was in the background as he was my senior and also the heir apparent. I would do odd tasks, but nothing of great consequence; even QRG had more faith in Ajesh's abilities than mine. QRG would later confess, 'Anil was too soft a manager in those days. He seemed disinterested in business. I was also more focused on Ajesh until he separated.'

But now QRG had no option. He had to depend on me, he had to push me as the second in command; slowly, his perceptions about me changed as I delivered results, and donned my elder brother's hat.

Third, the leadership confusion vanished. After May 1995, QRG was the decision taker; I was the next heir apparent but I worked in his shadow. The employees and other stakeholders realized who they had to talk to, and who they had to convince. The power structure was clear.

After the third family separation, QRG's empire was at around Rs 60–70 crore. We were largely into switchgears, as the bulk of the electric meters business went to my elder brother. However, with my father's entire focus on growth, we expanded rapidly.

As far as family was concerned, the relations remained cordial. Time, indeed, is the biggest healer. A few years ago, we all got involved in finding a match for Ajesh's daughter. Finally, things were the way everybody in the family had always wanted them to be.

TWELVE

Rebooting Havells

After the settlement with Ajesh, QRG understandably felt low—but not for long. This is a trait I often noticed in him. Nothing could hold his spirits down indefinitely. After every setback, professional or personal, he would rise Phoenix-like from the ashes. He would get some divine energy and he would bounce back with double the vigour.

This is the hallmark of a great leader. Gloom spreads easily. If the person at the top surrounds himself with hopelessness and negativity, the whole organization suffers. It is the job of the leader to radiate energy—under all circumstances. Setbacks and losses happen, but they can't derail a person or an organization.

At that time, QRG had another physical ailment—dry eye syndrome. It is an autoimmune disease caused by decreased tear production or faster evaporation of tears. It makes the eyes scratchy, itchy and dry. Even if a person wants to cry, tears don't roll out. Even a little bit of dust or bright lights would cause QRG immense pain.

But even that wasn't enough to put him out of action. About ten days after the split with Ajesh, QRG, wearing

dark glasses, came to the Havells office at Raj Narain Marg
in Civil Lines and called a meeting of the key executives.
His depression and pain were not on display. He said
Havells, which was then a Rs 60-crore company, should
strive to become a Rs 300-crore company in five years.

In other words, it should increase its current turnover
every year—for the next five years. The idea of this
ambitious target was to reassure all of us that Ajesh's exit
would change nothing. Everybody came out of the meeting
charged with energy. All doubts were cleared. Those who
had doubted QRG's resolve were proved wrong.

Now, QRG turned his attention to me. As Ajesh had
retained our old house, and our new house, also in Civil
Lines, was still under construction, we had moved to our
farmhouse at Mehrauli. During the hour-long commute to
office, QRG began discussing the intricacies of the business
with me.

His energy and enthusiasm were infectious. With QRG's
guidance, I too began to feel confident. A new energy
began to flow inside me. It was the kind of adrenaline rush
I had never felt in the three years after I had joined the
business in 1992. QRG turned my life around with his
magic touch. The hallmark of every great leader is that he
can get ordinary people to do extraordinary work.

In 1995, Havells had a sizeable switchgear business
and a small meter business. QRG felt that we should
identify new product lines if we were to grow rapidly. He
encouraged me to go to the market and see which products
were popular.

I did the rounds of our top dealers. We were a trade-
friendly company, and the idea was to assess which new

products we could launch through our dealer network. After extensive discussions, we decided to focus on two products—modular switches and moulded case circuit breakers, or MCCBs.

Modular switches were a new concept in the country. These were products for the next generation. Earlier, the market comprised piano switches, also called *khatka* switches, which were mounted on Bakelite panels. Anchor, a Mumbai-based company that was set up in 1963, was acquired by Panasonic Corporation of Japan in 2007 and had a virtual monopoly in this market. MK Electric, an English company that was formed in 1919 to make sockets, had started to sell modular switches in the country. While the piano switch sold for Rs 10, a modular switch was priced at Rs 50.

Always a believer in futuristic products, QRG thought we should pursue the opportunity. Since MK was an English company, we decided to look for a European partner for both modular switches and MCCBs (these are higher-capacity versions of MCBs).

On 3 June, barely a couple of weeks after Ajesh had moved out, I left for the United Kingdom, Italy and Germany on a fifteen-day trip to scout for a partner. My cousin Ameet, Surjitji's son, went with me. He had recently joined the business and QRG felt we would be able to work better together.

We met a host of companies and came back with some good leads. I followed it up with another fifteen-day trip in November. By February 1996, we had shortlisted two companies—Hanson Electricals and MEM, both based in Birmingham in the UK.

Hanson plc was an £11-billion conglomerate set up by James Hanson and Gordon White. The two had got into partnership in the sixties. They became famous in the seventies for buying distressed assets at low cost and then selling the assets for profit. 'They were often accused of "asset stripping" but in reality, their policy consisted of squeezing as much profit as possible out of the assets they had acquired, having sold off those which they deemed irrelevant,' the *Independent* wrote after Hanson's death in November 2004. 'They were so successful that Hanson was the first British businessman to earn over £1 million a year and he was once described as Europe's most potent capitalist.'

Hanson's biggest moment came in 1986 when he acquired Imperial Group, a British conglomerate with interests in food, tobacco and brewing, and a large pension fund. In 1991, he made a bid to acquire ICI, the chemicals group, but gave it up after it came to light that his partner, White, had used shareholders' money to bet on racehorses.

Outside the boardroom, Hanson led a colourful life. In the fifties, Hanson dated Jean Simmons and Joan Collins and was also engaged to Audrey Hepburn for a year. White's daughter was Sita White, the one-time girlfriend of former Pakistani cricketer, and now a political heavyweight in his country, Imran Khan. The dashing Pathan is known to have fathered her child.

Hanson plc had a company called Hanson Electricals that made modular switches under the Crabtree brand and MCCBs labelled Dorman Smith. Both the brands had considerable resonance in India. Dorman Smith was brought to India by a company called Morarji Dorman

Smith. It had done well and created strong equity for the brand. It was acquired by Legrand, the French switchgear giant, in 1995. Therefore, we preferred Hanson Electricals to MEM. Evolved customers had also heard of Crabtree switches.

Hanson plc too was interested in us, and so was MEM, because of our widespread distribution network. Perhaps they felt that they could leverage it to sell their products in large numbers in India, a key emerging market.

While we were mulling over these options, QRG said that we should also look at the meters business. This market was going through a metamorphosis. Till then, the country had used electromagnetic meters. Landis+Gyr, the Swiss meters giant which was founded in 1896, had brought electromechanical meters to India, which were made in its factory in Calcutta. State electricity boards were buying these meters in large numbers.

QRG said that since we were the largest player in this category of the meters business till 1995, we too should make new-age electromechanical meters in technical collaboration with some top-notch multinational corporation. QRG had, in the past, driven the meters business personally and therefore was keen to give it another go.

I made some inquiries and was told that it might be worthwhile to talk to DZG, a German metering company that was established in 1920 by Anton Stepper, a metering expert.

I sent a fax to the DZG head office at Hamburg (its factory was situated near Stuttgart), and was told that a top team of theirs was visiting Dubai where I could meet them. I left for the desert city right away to hold the first set of talks. The negotiations took off on a positive note.

As soon as I came back, QRG sprung a surprise on me.

In 1994, Guptajee & Co. had finally given up the agency for Fort Gloster Industries. The reason was that Havells required our full attention and we could obviously not do any justice to the cable and wire dealership. (We didn't close down the shop for sentimental reasons—after all, this is where the family began its entrepreneurial journey. We retain the shop to date. It sells Havells products. Every Diwali, we hold our first puja there.)

Now, QRG said we should get into the cable business once again and this time on our own. This was a business he knew really well, and hence it could be scaled up quickly. This was also the time that India had entered the real estate boom—the demand for cables and wire would only go northwards from here, he said.

QRG pitched for re-entering this business because he had seen an opening. Rajasthan State Industrial Development and Investment Corporation, or RIICO, had announced that it wanted to auction a cable and wire plant at Alwar. Surya Cables, the company that owned the plant, had not been able to pay the dues that RIICO now wanted to recover by auctioning the factory.

We all went to Alwar, which is located a few hours from Delhi, to see the unit. By then, QRG had hired an expert in cable and wire production, O.P. Kawatra, for advice. He had once worked for Fort Gloster Industries and that's how QRG knew him and of his technical expertise. However, Kawatra was down with fever and could not accompany us.

The plant was locked and we learnt that it was mothballed around two years ago. There was no guard but we were unable to look inside. But QRG did not need any further inspection. 'I have seen the Fort Gloster Industries plant. Let's take this one,' he announced with finality.

Our internal calculations indicated we could pay up to Rs 1.6 crore, which was the base price. Our team for the auction, led by CFO Rajesh Gupta, was given this price mandate. Unfortunately, there was another interested party and, therefore, a bidding war ensued. The price went up to Rs 1.8 crore. Our finance team was in a quandary.

The price had overshot their mandate. But QRG had also told them that they should not miss this opportunity. The team members had no mobile phones, although cellular phones had been launched by then, to get in touch with us. They continued to bid. Finally, we won the bid at Rs 2.1 crore. Our team was both elated and scared. Would QRG be happy or angry? How would we justify a payment almost a third more than the mandate?

With elation and trepidation in equal measure in their hearts, the team came back to Delhi. I remember I was a bit piqued but my father was comfortable. His calculations were based on Kawatra's assurance that the unit could generate revenues of Rs 1 crore a month at full capacity. So, an additional Rs 50 lakh to acquire the unit was not a problem. QRG never let niggles such as these make him lose sight of the big picture.

The built-up area of the Alwar plant was five acres. After the purchase, QRG was asked if he would wish to buy another seven and a half acres, adjacent to the factory. Most business persons would have turned down the offer.

They would have argued that the business plan entailed five acres and, thus, there was no need to spend more to buy another seven and a half acres. But QRG agreed, despite the fact that we had just paid Rs 50 lakh more than our internal estimate at the auction. Again, he was thinking long term. He was ahead of the curve compared to all of us.

Both decisions turned out to be prescient. QRG's instincts were proved right when Fort Gloster Industries, now under the control of S.K. Bangur, asked us to become its vendor in north India to supply cables. This meant we would have to produce under their brand, not Havells. This was against QRG's usual style but he agreed because we were also expanding into switches, MCCBs and meters at that time, and our hands were full.

Since the arrangement guaranteed some returns, we agreed. Disaster struck a year later, when the cables industry collapsed and the Bangurs walked out of the outsourcing arrangement. While this would have made others redraw their plans, QRG did not worry too much about the fallout, and launched the Havells brand of cables.

Luck favours the brave. Our cables were an instant success. We were able to utilize the entire twelve and a half acres of land within four years. Today, the Alwar plant is spread over 100 acres. From Rs 1 crore a month, it does a turnover of over Rs 200 crore a month.

That was quintessential QRG—when most people would listen to an idea and question why, he would turn around and say why not.

In the first week of March 1996, I was scheduled to visit Birmingham to finalize the joint venture with either

Hanson plc or MEM. Days before that, an internal discussion started—as we had just bought a unit and got into a new business, should we rush headlong into another new segment? Wouldn't it be prudent to consolidate the cable business first and then look at modular switches and MCCBs?

These arguments were not without merit, though it was not about the money. We were, at that time, still a small company with limited managerial bandwidth; it would be unwise to spread it too thinly over several businesses. That's what conventional wisdom suggested, and many of us were in agreement with that. The final decision was left to QRG.

By now, he had developed great confidence in me. He asked me what we should do. I said, 'Let me travel to Birmingham and see how it goes. We can take a decision after we know what's on the table.' We had, after all, made no commitments till then. QRG agreed. To me, he looked tentative and non-committal. Maybe he was testing us to see if we had the appetite to think and act big.

Ameet travelled with me. In Birmingham, we went to Hanson plc first. Our first meeting was with David Norman, the managing director of Hanson Electricals, which was a unit of Hanson plc. As our luggage hadn't arrived, we turned up for the meeting in denims and T-shirts. The Hanson team wore dark suits and ties. At first sight, they must have thought that we were not serious about the whole affair. What worked in our favour was that Norman had visited India a few years ago and had heard good things about the Havells distribution network.

Without much ado, he said he wanted to form a joint venture with Havells where his company would own 51 per cent—a controlling stake.

This, I told him as politely as I could, was unacceptable to us, and that we'd be happy to do a 50-50 partnership. Norman immediately spoke to his CEO, Chris Thomas, and then said that equal ownership was fine with him. I told him that I had to meet another company in two days, and hence wanted them to be absolutely sure. Norman said he had the memorandum of understanding ready.

I called up QRG from Birmingham and broke the news to him. This time, there was no vacillation. In unequivocal terms, he asked me to go ahead and sign on the dotted line. And that's precisely what I did.

But I didn't want to tell MEM. I spent two days with that company, knowing very well that I had to go through the motions. Those were the two dreariest days of my life.

I returned to India. And in June 1996, the joint venture agreement was finally signed. Hanson's son, Robert, came to Delhi for the event. Apart from other things, we treated him to a hearty Indian meal at Bukhara, the restaurant in the ITC Maurya that was later made famous by the Clintons.

The new company was called Havells Dorman Smith and it introduced two brands in the market in 1997—Crabtree for modular switches and Dorman Smith for MCCBs. We made Crabtree switches at Gurgaon, and for MCCBs, we set up a new line at our motor control gear factory at Faridabad.

But things move fast in business, often in ways one does not anticipate. The year it signed the agreement with us,

Hanson plc got divided into four. It decided to divest itself of Hanson Electricals. Chris Thomas, the CEO of Hanson Electrics, was an old company hand. He had started his career with Crabtree and had grown steadily to run the business. He was also very smart. He led a management buyout of Hanson Electricals and renamed it Electrium.

The change meant nothing to us, and it was business as usual. Sometime in 2000, we got a communication from Electrium that it wanted to cash out of the joint venture, ostensibly under pressure from their private equity investors. Since we had the right of first refusal, they offered their stake to us first.

We didn't have much of a choice, really. Both the brands were doing well. QRG told us not to debate the issue, and just pay them the right price. His idea was to ensure that the business, which was growing steadily, should witness no disruption. So, we did three things—one, we bought Electrium's 50 per cent stake; two, we changed the MCCB brand from Havells Dorman Smith to Havells; and three, we bought the rights for Crabtree for the entire Indian subcontinent.

We made these purchases at book value. We paid Rs 2.5 crore for Electrium's stake and another Rs 2.5 crore for the Crabtree rights. (It proved to be an excellent purchase— the brand now has an annual turnover of Rs 200 crore and a net profit of almost Rs 40 crore.) Thomas, once again, proved his efficiency—the whole deal was wrapped up in three hours.

While signing the agreement for Crabtree, QRG made sure it was foolproof. 'Bring back the sale deed yourself, do not courier it,' his instructions to me were very clear. Of course, he preferred short agreements that were watertight and not open to interpretation by some smart lawyer.

Electrium wasn't sure this deal would go through smoothly. Its investors had warned the firm that it was very difficult, if not impossible, to take money out of India. Indeed, many a foreign company had found to its chagrin that Indian partners did not conduct a break-up in a professional and amicable manner. When our deal concluded without a hitch, Electrium was pleasantly surprised.

That ended one relationship with Hanson Electricals/ Electrium. But I had become good friends with Thomas. After the split, he decided to buy MCBs made by us for sale in overseas markets. That was a huge show of confidence in us and in the capability of our factories. It also gave us some exposure to the international market that would come in handy one day. Our paths would cross once again in life, but we will come to that later.

At the time of tying up with Hanson Electricals, we came in touch with Coopers & Lybrand, the professional services that were hired by the English company to facilitate the discussions. It would later become a part of PricewaterhouseCoopers, or PwC.

Two years later, the PwC partners who had worked on the deal, Timmy Kandhari and Rajiv Goel, approached us with an offer. We had four operating companies—Havells India, Havells Industries, Havells Dorman Smith and Towers & Transformers. There were some crossholdings too. Why don't you consolidate the companies and have a simple structure, they suggested.

Your fees, we asked. We will take Rs 50 lakh for this, the two said. For me, this was a big expense. I happened to mention the proposal to QRG. He asked me how we would benefit from this. I rattled them out—synergies in operations, saving in costs, better value, etc. His response was simple, 'Okay, let's do it.' When I mentioned the fees, he was fine with that, too.

That was an eye-opener for me. If there is value in an offer, QRG didn't worry too much about the price. In his mind, QRG had done a cost-benefit analysis and decided that the benefits far outweighed the cost. Yet again, he taught us not to miss the woods for a misshapen tree. PwC was on board. As a result, we now have two companies— QRG Enterprises, the family holding company, and Havells India, the operating company. A rather complex structure morphed into a simple one.

Around the same time that we had got into cables and wire, modular switches and MCCBs, we finalized our partnership with DZG. The German company was insistent on a fifty-fifty venture with us. But we offered it another deal. Since we were already doing meters in Towers & Transformers, we felt DZG should take a stake in that company.

At that time, meters were sold to state electricity boards. Towers & Transformers already had those connections. If a new company were to be set up, it would have to build those competencies from scratch. It was like reinventing the wheel. But if we made the new meters in Towers & Transformers, we would be able to cut the go-to-market time and get started almost instantly. DZG saw merit in our suggestion and bought 7 per cent in that company.

What helped was that the DZG CEO, Karl-Heinz Paasch, was an easy-going person. We hit it off quite well. He was so busy that he could find the time to come to India on weekends only.

The new unit was set up in Sahibabad—on the vacant land in the Towers & Transformers plot—at a cost of Rs 35 crore. This was our largest investment so far in manufacturing.

QRG was insistent that the factory should be the gold standard in meters in the country. He used to tell us that we must set up a German factory in India. So, we gave the German technicians a free hand, and QRG told the Indian engineers and technicians that they should become their students for at least two years. Even the machines were imported from Germany.

QRG knew this was a sensitive matter and needed to be handled with care. It would have been naive on our part to assume that the Indian engineers and technicians would agree to play a secondary role without kicking up a fuss. But QRG ensured that their protests did not impact his plans.

Sometime in 1999, the new meters, branded Havells DZG, were out in the market. They sold at 100 per cent premium over all existing meters.

These meters helped QRG achieve what he had set out to achieve five years earlier. By 2000, he had set the target of Rs 300 crore in turnover. With the booming meters business, we hit Rs 400 crore by that year. More importantly, Havells had in this time expanded into cable and wire, modular switches, MCCBs and electromechanical meters. Those who had doubted QRG's conviction and persistence were proved wrong.

The only piece of the jigsaw puzzle that was still missing was multi-functional meters, which are meant for industrial use. At the time, there were four companies making them in India—Larsen & Toubro, ABB, Secure Meters and Duke Arnics. The last of these, Duke Arnics, was a small company with a turnover of Rs 10–15 crore. We decided to acquire it from its technocrat promoter, Dr D.N. Rao, for an enterprise value of Rs 10 crore to get into multi-functional meters. Thus, in April 2000, we acquired 60 per cent of it.

Rao, when he came to sign the deal, told QRG that his ambition was that he should drive around in a Mercedes. We all found it a little strange, especially because the price of the deal was already agreed, but QRG thought nothing of it and gave Rao the car of his dreams. We acquired the rest of the company in 2003 and merged it into Towers & Transformers. Its plant and technology were transferred to our factory at Sahibabad.

All was going well, except that QRG lost his mentor, O.P. Gupta, to cancer. Over the years, the two had got closer and closer. They used to call each other at 5.45 a.m. every day and talk for 15 minutes—long-distance call rates were a quarter before 6 a.m. They used to discuss everything under the sun—family, business, films, food, books—no subject was taboo. The two families used to take vacations together.

In the early years, O.P. Gupta used to take his family to one hill station or the other during the Durga puja holidays in Calcutta. During those days, he used to call QRG over to handle his business. For a long time, QRG had the authority to sign cheques on O.P. Gupta's behalf. Their relationship was marked by love, respect, understanding and trust.

In March 1999, O.P. Gupta was diagnosed with cancer. QRG flew to Calcutta and went straight from the airport to the nursing home where his uncle was admitted. In September, QRG came to know of a top nephrologist in Mumbai and arranged for me to take him to Calcutta to see O.P. Gupta.

One day, O.P. Gupta, who had perhaps sensed that the end had come, told QRG that he wanted to meet his elder brother Lekh Raj Gupta's widow, Kaushalya, whom he used to hold in high esteem for her guts and pluck. QRG immediately took her to Calcutta where she got to spend a few days with O.P. Gupta.

After O.P. Gupta passed away in 2000, his son, Vickyji, kept up the routine of daily morning conversations with QRG. He would one day become an associate director of Havells. Vickyji was given the responsibility to develop the eastern market for Havells—West Bengal, Bihar, Jharkhand, Orissa, Sikkim, the Northeast and Bhutan.

THIRTEEN

Jallandhar King

At the turn of the century, QRG was sixty-three. At that age, most people lose all appetite for work and begin to plan their retirement. Not QRG—he was as excited about business as a child. In spite of his severe health problems, most notably rheumatoid arthritis and dry eye syndrome, it seemed that nothing could slow him down. By 2000, our appetite for growth had increased manifold.

There was also the confidence that we could digest acquisitions. Apart from Towers & Transformers and Duke Arnics, in 1997 we acquired a Noida-based company called Electric Control & Switchboard that made panels to house MCBs and MCCBs from one K.C. Agarwal for Rs 3 crore. We bought it because even Larsen & Toubro had a similar business.

But we realized in no time that it was a low-technology product, which meant the profit margins were very slim. The payment cycle of up to 150 days was unusually long. Also, we could not sell it through our existing network of distributors. So, in a short span of time, we mothballed this business.

We were now on the lookout for a bigger acquisition—one that would help us leapfrog over rivals in the marketplace. Several names would get discussed in the morning meetings but nothing fruitful came up. Then, one day, somebody mentioned Standard Electricals.

This was a company that had been in operation since 1956. There were four founders—J.K. Gupta, J.M. Goyal, V.P. Mahendroo and Ajit Ranade. The company made switchgear for industrial as well as domestic use at its factory in Jallandhar in Punjab. Until the nineties, it was bigger than Havells and a very respected name in the business.

During the years of Punjab militancy, Mahendroo and Ranade had relocated to Delhi to look after market development. Eventually, in 1990, the two opted out and started their own company called Indo-Asian Fusegear. Standard Electricals was now owned by J.K. Gupta and J.M. Goyal.

Somebody pointed out to us that both the promoters had daughters, and would therefore not mind selling off the company. It was a sad commentary on gender inequality in the corporate world, but it was the bitter truth. Today, there are quite a few businessmen who have inducted their daughters into business—Adi Godrej, Prathap Reddy, Analjit Singh and Kishore Biyani, among others. At that time, especially in the extremely patriarchal northern India, businesses were passed on only to male heirs.

We were definitely interested in Standard Electricals. The company had a strong brand, Standard, which was once bigger and stronger than Havells. It was felt that a two-brand strategy would work well for us. Standard would give us new markets and distribution channels. For instance, it was strong in the south where we were weak. Its factory at Jallandhar was said to be better than the Havells switchgear factories at Kirti Nagar and Badli in Delhi.

In several ways, Standard Electricals was a good fit with Havells. Instinctively, QRG dialled J.K. Gupta in Jallandhar and said the two of them should meet whenever he was next in Delhi.

J.K. Gupta was a man of style. Because of his regal bearing and his fondness for luxury cars, people often called him the Jallandhar King. He used to drive a Toyota Lexus, which was a big deal in those days.

Two or three weeks later, J.K. Gupta came to meet QRG at our office at Raj Narain Marg. Once the pleasantries were over, QRG said that since both of them were in switchgear, why not work together? To QRG's surprise, this is precisely what J.K. Gupta too had in mind. 'Before I left home this morning, I had told my wife that even if I have to sell my company today, I will do that.'

Instead, QRG proposed a joint venture—there was no talk of acquiring Standard Electricals, not yet. J.K. Gupta was eager and wanted to thrash out the details of the arrangement immediately. QRG suggested they leave the nitty-gritty to the professionals. He then called up Timmy Kandhari and Rajiv Goel at PwC and asked them to see him in fifteen minutes. The two were surprised but nevertheless made it to our office on time. During the conversations, QRG asked them how the deal should be structured if Havells were to take 51 per cent. Slowly, but very steadily, QRG had eased J.K. Gupta into the deal.

J.K. Gupta had put a value of Rs 25 crore on his company, and that's the figure he mentioned to QRG. Again, QRG said he would leave it to Kandhari and Goel to figure that out. On their advice, after they had done their due diligence, QRG told J.K. Gupta that the enterprise value of Standard Electricals should be Rs 18 crore, which included Rs 3 crore of debt. J.K. Gupta and his partner, J.M. Goyal, agreed and we paid them around Rs 8.5 crore for a 60 per cent stake in Standard Electricals.

But, before long, trouble erupted. J.K. Gupta and J.M. Goyal were under the impression that in spite of our majority stake, they would continue to run the factory, while we took care of marketing and distribution. This is not what we had in mind—we wanted complete control of the company. But perhaps we did not convey this aspect to them properly.

This was a big lesson we learnt. In our bid to close the deal quickly, we had overlooked this vital communication. We thought that since we had taken a controlling stake, it went without saying that we would run the company, but we ought to have done it better. In the niceties of the talk, this important aspect was inadvertently ignored. Both J.K. Gupta and J.M. Goyal were very nice people, so perhaps we did not feel the need for any tough talking.

In hindsight, it was clear that we ought to have laid all the cards on the table politely—that would have driven the message home without causing them any offence. One can be firm without being unpleasant. It was an oversight and we paid the price for it. Within a year, it was clear to us that such a state of affairs could not last for long.

It soon escalated into a fully fledged corporate battle. Our managers tried to enter the Jallandhar factory to take over the operations. But Standard Electricals' executives fought back and drove us out of the premises. The case went to the Company Law Board as we tried to seek a legal remedy.

However, QRG was not happy with the legal mess. Throughout his life, he had depended on personal relationships and negotiations to settle any difficulties in business. Even the three separations within the family had not gone to the courts—they had been settled over glasses of lassi. While many of us weren't averse to a full-blown legal fight, because we were convinced that our case was strong, QRG wanted a peaceful settlement out of court. He somehow felt that the other side was also not wrong. The spat hadn't made him lose his sense of balance.

There was a clause in the agreement that we could raise our stake in Standard Electricals from 60 per cent to 100 per cent at a predetermined price. When we tried to invoke the clause, J.K. Gupta resisted it. It was a stalemate when hearings began in the Company Law Board.

This was not to QRG's liking. He knew the legal battle was a waste of resources. So, QRG insisted that we should settle the matter out of court, even if it meant that we had to pay more.

The challenge was to convey this to J.K. Gupta. By now, things were so bad that there was no communication between us at all. Finally, QRG identified a gentleman with the surname Chhibber, who was a childhood friend of J.K. Gupta and was also the lawyer representing him. He had come to know that J.K. Gupta would often pay heed to Chhibber's words. It was a slim chance and QRG grabbed it with both hands. He convinced Chhibber that a settlement was the right thing to do, and asked him to intervene and resolve the issue.

This was easier said than done. J.K. Gupta was clearly feeling very hurt and was not prepared for any out-of-court settlement. Finally, Chhibber also gave up and told QRG that all his efforts were futile.

All seemed lost. But QRG was the eternal optimist. He requested Chhibber to talk to J.K. Gupta one last time. Fortunately, this time J.K. Gupta agreed but he wanted a higher price. Under the agreement, we were supposed to pay him and J.M. Goyal, Rs 5.5 crore for the residual 40 per cent stake. But we had to pay him a lot more than that. Again, QRG didn't mind—it was a small price to pay for resolving the mess and for peace of mind.

The final deal was signed on 31 December 2001. After nine months of negotiations, which often looked pointless and hopeless, we had succeeded in acquiring Standard Electricals fully. We were now indisputably in control.

In MCBs, our market share was 13–14 per cent. With the purchase of Standard Electricals, it shot up to 16–18 per cent. We became the third largest player in the market after Legrand and Indo-Asian Fusegear. Havells would overtake all of them to become the market leader in 2004–05.

Havells's story so far had been one of growth and acquisitions. It was now set to take a new turn.

Stever Robbins, the veteran of nine start-up companies and a venture coach, who advises early-stage companies, wrote in one of his columns, 'It is not enough to build a business worth a fortune; you have to make sure you have an exit strategy, a way to get the money back out.'

The same article describes five primary exit strategies for entrepreneurs—bleed the company dry on a daily basis, liquidate the company when enough is enough, sell the firm to a friendly buyer, get acquired by a bigger corporation, and plan an IPO (initial public offering) to reduce your equity.

However, even an expert like Robbins forgot about two other typical business situations. What should an entrepreneur do when his business crashes because of internal and/or external reasons? Logically, some of the five plans can work in such instances too, like liquidate, bleed the company and sell it to a friendly acquirer. But what if an entrepreneur decides to deliberately close down a business? He does not wish to sell or liquidate, just wind it down.

For most businessmen, the last one is not an option. Who would want to close down an existing, profitable division without realizing whatever value is available in the marketplace? Why would one bear a complete loss if the business is up and running but has a bleak future? Why not just put it in the lap of another business person, who can take the decision in the future?

That's where QRG was different from most entrepreneurs. In the past, he deliberately got out of the meters business, which he thought would not be sustainable after a few years. He did not sell it, he did not allow it to go bankrupt; he merely wound it down, steadily, over a few years.

The nineties witnessed huge reforms in several sectors, especially the power sector. Multinational corporations lined up to invest in seemingly lucrative projects in India. In 1991, the Private Power Policy opened up the path to private and foreign investment in the generation and distribution of electricity. The policy framework was further strengthened through the introduction of the Mega Power Policy in 1995. This was revised in 1998 and a number of fiscal incentives were added.

The worst area for reforms was the state electricity boards. Although they had a majority share in generation of electricity and were able to monopolize distribution, they were in a financial mess. According to a 2006 report of the power ministry, 'By the nineties, the state electricity boards were found to be beset by unsustainable inefficiencies, unviable tariffs, high transmission and distribution losses, mounting subsidies, lack of adequate attention to the distribution system, sub-optimal performance, wasteful practices and lackadaisical financial management.' All this led to the financial fragility of the entire sector.

Due to the uninspiring financial position of the vertically integrated monolithic state electricity boards, the power sector was failing to attract the much-needed investment for its development. Power sector reforms were necessitated to turn around the sector. Orissa was the first state to restructure its electricity board and, thereafter, twelve states followed suit.

The World Bank stepped in to help in the restructuring of the state electricity boards. Apart from consultancy and white papers, it committed huge funds to several state electricity boards. As a result, the business of meters boomed in the late nineties. Havells was at the right place at the right time, with its tentacles spread majorly in several states—Andhra Pradesh, Karnataka, Tamil Nadu, Punjab, Jammu and Kashmir, Uttar Pradesh, Madhya Pradesh, Rajasthan and Haryana.

From Rs 60 crore in 1998, the meters division contributed Rs 300 crore to the annual turnover in 2002, or over 60 per cent of the group's turnover. Its contribution to our profit was even higher. We were possibly the largest player in this segment.

Obviously, there was internal, as well as external (shareholders, especially institutional ones) pressure on us to develop this business. Unfortunately, the dynamics of the business changed almost overnight.

By 2000, it was evident that there was a shift in technology. The World Bank, as well as the other funders and state electricity boards, decided to replace the existing electromechanical meters with electronic ones. This was to make the meters tamper-proof and facilitate easy billings. These meters were considered more fashionable, though there were no practical benefits.

While electromechanical meters were really high-tech products, electronic meters were just a printed circuit board, or PCB, housed in a box. They were easy and inexpensive to produce. Overnight, a large number of meter companies flooded the market. Prices began to crash.

At the same time, the norms of the business took a turn for the worse. Meters were bought by the state electricity boards. Till then, orders were placed, by and large, on merit. Bribery was minimal. Towards the end of the nineties, the whole culture of kickbacks and commissions came into play in a big way. It is generally regarded as the time when the politician–businessman nexus reached its nadir. In the absence of transparent guidelines, kickbacks reached new heights—across sectors.

In meters too one had to be in constant touch with the political masters. In some states, the powers brokers would openly ask for a commission of 5 per cent on orders. At the same time, as the World Bank was funding the switch to electric meters, the orders became huge—almost ten times the earlier ones. As a result, kickbacks also increased tenfold.

On paper, the state electricity boards gave orders to the lowest bidders. But the guidelines about qualifications for the bid were left murky and open to manipulation. Worse, many companies were ready to pay kickbacks. We were distinctly uncomfortable with all this.

The boom in the business had attracted a host of new players, most of whom were smaller upstarts, who wanted to grab the business at any cost. They were even willing to sell at a small loss in order to gain market share. Suddenly, prices slid and margins grew wafer thin in most cases, and disappeared in some instances.

Havells had to make choices. First, it had to invest huge amounts in the new electronics technology. Second, it had to compete fiercely to retain its market share, forget about expanding the business. Finally, it had to sell at low margins or at a loss. We knew that these smaller players would find it difficult to remain in business, but we had no idea when this would happen.

Should Havells sink in investments without knowing when, or if at all, it would yield profitable returns? Should the company remain in the meters business at all?

QRG felt we shouldn't. His logic was that the new business dynamics did not gel with the DNA of the group. We did not have the skills to be successful in a corrupt market. He believed that it was better to spend money to develop the other businesses rather than continue in meters. It was a huge decision—we had to let go of our most successful enterprise.

In 2003, QRG announced that the meters business would be wound down. We stopped taking fresh orders. The old orders, for which we had furnished bank guarantees, would be met. We didn't want to be seen as bad vendors. By 2006–07, the meters business was gone. The brand new machinery that we had put up at Sahibabad was sold as scrap. Towers & Transformers was merged into QRG Enterprises, the holding company.

QRG was not blind to the human cost of this drastic step. After all, there were many people who worked there. Fortunately, the meters business was production led. The buyers were mostly state electricity boards and the top managers would liaise with them. There was not a large field force to market the meters.

Once QRG decided to exit the meters business, he announced that we would set up a switchgear factory at the same site. Most of the workers and technicians would be absorbed there. For reskilling, we sent many of them to our switchgear unit at Faridabad. That's how human cost was kept down to almost zero. Some people were also absorbed in the cable business, where again, government departments were large buyers.

QRG took such unconventional and bold decisions several times, or at least threatened to do so. This was the advice he gave to his senior managers on a regular basis—if a business is not worth it, does not fit in with our corporate philosophy, and we don't have the expertise to manage it, it is better to shut it down. There are two advantages to such a management approach. The managers may agree with this line of thinking and the company can cut down its future losses and avoid loss of face. Or the head of the specific division would be shaken up, engage in healthy discussions, and go all out to turn it around. Either way, the company remains the beneficiary.

Whenever QRG encountered corruption in an institutionalized and systemic manner, he shied away from it. He was as honest as the system would allow him to be, and he would not be a part of an overriding system of corruption. He preferred to close down a lucrative and profitable division once corruption increased manifold and became unmanageable.

'Right from the sixties, I had told my managers and other employees not to be corrupt. Business houses that became corrupt, and where personal materialism became important, have vanished over the years. Even some of the bigger firms that rotted in this manner are gone. In the long run, successful businesses are built on corporate ethics and values,' QRG would say later.

The biggest advantage of this personal integrity was that he could delegate responsibilities to others. If a business organization is inherently and deliberately corrupt, the owner would wish to oversee everything that happens in the company. Failing that, he would have to entrust all responsibilities to a few loyalists, who would report directly to him.

Such a corporate structure is distorted and crumbles quickly, especially when the business expands. Lack of delegation is the biggest enemy of efficient organizations and cripples most companies. But even as a trader, QRG had no qualms about delegating responsibilities. In fact, he was rarely in the office.

Naturally, this led to a more professional organization. Without knowing the management theories behind it, QRG knew the benefits of a professional culture in a company.

'As I delegated, I understood I had more time to think of growth, meet people outside, and expand the business. Thus, my focus shifted to the future potential, rather than looking at the present. If I stayed in the office or the shop, I knew I could make Rs 100, which could come down to Rs 90 if I delegated the job.

'But because I had more time, I could expand the business to Rs 150 in no time. And there was always a fair chance that the manager whom I had entrusted the responsibility to would learn the tricks of the trade and add to the overall growth in the near future,' QRG would say.

This invariably led QRG to learn the art and science of how to manage people. Since he didn't come from a professional background, he had to hire people who were engineers, finance graduates and marketers, when he got into manufacturing. He did not know the intricacies of these fields.

Business persons the world over generally do not get into the minute details of any business; unless, of course, they are professionals, as is the case today in sectors such as financial services and information technology.

'What did the Munjals know about cycles or motorcycles, when they set up those businesses? Or the Tatas when they envisaged a giant steel plant? The trick was to find the right professionals, and delegate responsibilities to them. If you did that, they would deliver results,' QRG would often say.

'Business persons who micromanage every decision do not grow much. In my case, the idea to delegate was natural. I had also met senior managers in other companies and I realized how businesses were managed. They were run by professionals and any entrepreneur had to have faith in them. All big businesses are finally run by skilled professionals, not by the owners,' QRG would say.

Willy-nilly, in an era when managers had little idea about corporate governance and business ethics, QRG built an organization whose foundations were built on such sound principles.

FOURTEEN

Nothing but the Best

With meters out of the way, we began to think of new products. The idea was: How could we leverage our distribution network to sell more products? One option was fans.

In 2001, we set up a small team under B.K. Gupta, a veteran of the fan industry, to study the prospects and devise our entry strategy. The feedback we got from everybody was that it was not a great space to be in. There were six brands in the market—Crompton, Usha, Bajaj, Orient, Polar and Khaitan. No new brand had come up in the last twenty-five years. That was because the unorganized sector had a huge presence in the market. These small-time factories thrived on evasion of excise duty and inferior material, and hence sold at rock-bottom prices. As a result, profit margins were wafer thin. Everybody advised us against entering the fan market.

QRG reasoned that the wire market had been similar, but we had entered it and done rather well for ourselves. The unorganized sector controlled 75 per cent of the cables market, and there was only one national brand, Finolex, though there were regional brands like Plaza and Kalinga in the north. And profit margins were almost non-existent.

In spite of these odds, we had become the second largest player in the market, after Finolex, in a few years. There was no reason, QRG believed, that we couldn't replicate that success in fans. But his condition was that we should make high-end fans which, backed by a strong brand, would simply fly off the shelves.

By now, Havells had fairly strong brand equity—it had come to be associated with high quality. QRG knew we had a great asset in the brand, and he understood its DNA fairly well. He may not have had a management degree under his belt, but QRG knew the essence of branding.

The naysayers felt he had lost it. Price was the name of the game. That was also the time the threat of inexpensive fans imported from China loomed over the Indian industry. The experts we had appointed also wanted us to make inexpensive fans. The USP of fans, in their scheme of things, was their price tag—the lower the better.

But QRG wouldn't budge. In the end, the China threat remained just a threat. Its ceiling fans couldn't create a dent in the Indian market, though it dominated in the table, pedestal and wall-mounted fan categories. Even that didn't last long. In a matter of years, Indians were able to wrest that market from the Chinese.

While he was absorbed in various serious issues, from fans to the legal wrangles over Standard Electricals, QRG's health suffered. In the earlier days, he had led an active life. He was fond of badminton and would go out for long walks in the morning with his friends from Civil Lines. But his health was fragile. In September 1995, he suffered a major heart attack. We rushed him from the farm to the hospital. That was the day when the whole country was witnessing the miracle of Ganesh idols consuming copious quantities of milk. Doctors decided not to do an angiography, but kept him on medication.

QRG had the habit of taking a bath right after his morning exercises. He never waited for the sweat to dry. My mother suspected that this had caused the rheumatoid arthritis, though it is an autoimmune disease, and she forbade us from following his example—we follow this instruction till date.

Due to the rheumatoid arthritis, QRG had got the dry eye syndrome. Because there wasn't enough lubrication in the eyes, he would need to put artificial tears every few minutes for the rest of his life. However, from 1996, the year my grandfather died, whenever he had extreme redness and pain, QRG had to keep his eyes padded up, at times for up to fifteen days. Sometimes, he used to have meetings in the office with the lights off to restrict the glare.

In 2001, his vision became extremely blurred. We consulted many doctors. Even the famous Sankar Netralaya in Chennai could not diagnose the problem. All of them said that it was not due to cataract. However, Mahipal Sachdeva of the Centre for Sight in Delhi performed a cataract operation and that helped him see 50–60 per cent better. But for the rest of his life, his sight was never 100 per cent. Because of this, he began to curtail his social life.

In 1999, again due to the rheumatoid arthritis, QRG developed interstitial lung disease, which reduces the lung capacity, makes the patient highly infection prone, and despite taking all precautions, the victim leads a tough life of generally not more than three to five years. It results in increased breathlessness and infections.

Doctors advised him to forget the rheumatoid arthritis and focus on the interstitial lung disease. They told him not to hold large meetings, and meet fewer and fewer people. But they could not stop him. Not only did he live for another fifteen years, but he raised the company's turnover from Rs 200 crore to Rs 8000 crore during that period!

In November 2001, QRG was admitted to Apollo Hospital in Delhi after he was diagnosed with double pneumonia. He later developed complications and contracted septicaemia. Also called sepsis, it is triggered by an infection. The infection is usually bacterial, but can also be fungal or viral. It is serious and can be life threatening as well. QRG spent eight to ten days in the intensive care unit. The symptoms were bad and the doctors gave him less than 50 per cent chances of survival.

One day at the ICU, even though he could barely speak, he told me, 'Let's not do fans right now.' Even in that state, his mind was ticking away. The seriousness of the situation, and the enormity of the ailment, had no impact on his mind. Most others would have been a bundle of nerves. QRG was made of sterner stuff.

I asked him not to worry and we would discuss the matter once he was back from the hospital. But it seemed he had used the time in the hospital to think it over and had made up his mind. 'These people (the team tasked to devise our fan strategy) are nowhere close to the vision I have. We will revisit it in some time,' he told me.

His voice may have been weak but the note of finality was unmistakable.

Once he was discharged from the hospital, QRG came to the office first before going home. There, in the presence of all the senior executives, he said, 'Let's shelve the project.' This came as a bit of a shock to most people. The team had located factories in India as well as China and was raring to go. B.K. Gupta, the team leader, was very confident about the foray. His only reservation was that the industry was very competitive and hence the focus should be on price—a view that QRG didn't subscribe to. Given a good product, QRG was convinced buyers wouldn't mind paying more. QRG's announcement that day dented all the plans drawn up by B.K. Gupta and his team.

Many a time, when QRG was not convinced about the workability of a plan, he would scrap it altogether and go back to square one. This is a trait I noticed in him time and again. Most people are happy to modify the plan here and there to make it work. But QRG would have none of it. So many times, he would simply start afresh. He was never the one to compromise and settle for anything that was not the best.

About a year later, we came to know of an opportunity in the fan market.

Gulshan Kumar was born into an ordinary household. His family ran a fruit juice kiosk in Daryaganj in Delhi. He got into making inexpensive music cassettes under the label T-Series, which flooded the market and took the established players by surprise. Through sheer hard work, by the mid-nineties, he was a leading player in the music industry. His rags-to-riches story was told and retold several times in the media.

Then, in 1997, an assassin shot him dead outside a temple in Mumbai. The business devolved on his son,

Bhushan Kumar, who was just a teenager at that time. During his father's time, the family had diversified into several unrelated areas like televisions, packaged water and fans. None of these met with the same success as the music cassettes. Today, Bhushan Kumar has transformed T-Series into the most potent force in the Indian music industry. He is also an immensely successful film producer.

We were informed by the distributors that T-Series fans were of high quality. However, buyers had not embraced them. Our ears perked up. We saw the fan factory at Noida and were fairly impressed with it. We met the finance director of the group and offered to acquire the factory.

While this was going on, QRG was thinking of erecting a brand new factory to make world-class fans.

For every task, QRG would hire specialists. For the proposed unit, we met M.L. Bhattar, who must have been close to seventy at that time, and was responsible for setting up many fan units in the country. QRG and I met him at the Oberoi in early 2003. Bhattar, in spite of his advanced years, was interested and said he wanted to put up one more factory before calling it quits—especially like the one we had in our cross hairs. He had saved the best for the last.

We acquired a ten-acre plot at Haridwar for the fan unit. The machinery installed was the best in the world. The tool room equipment came from Germany. The raw material we got—especially aluminium for the body— was the best available in the market. It was a totally integrated plant.

Until the time the Haridwar factory went on stream, we fed the market through the T-Series factory in Noida which we had acquired for just Rs 3–4 crore. It gave us a strong start—when Haridwar went into production, the distribution network was already firmly in place.

The major disruption that my father introduced in the fan segment was by rewriting the pricing rules of the game. While most manufacturers sold on the basis of as low a price as possible, we opted for premium pricing. Our prices were the same as that of the market leader, Crompton, owned by Gautam Thapar. We had steered clear of the economy segment.

Everyone advised QRG it was the wrong strategy. Internally, many managers felt that the trick was to compete on prices. Almost all the dealers we discussed this with advised us to enter the fan segment by launching low-priced economy variants.

But QRG was firm. He said he would offer the best-quality product at a premium price. His strategy worked because the consumers had changed in the twenty-first century. With an increasing ability to spend, the Indian consumer wanted the best, and she was willing to pay a higher price for it. She also wanted things to be different with USPs. Havells's fans gave her that.

At the launch conference, most of our 400-odd distributors and dealers predicted that we would fail unless we introduced low-priced fans. Our senior managers felt the same. At the press conference, QRG almost admonished the doubting Thomases. He did not wish to be a follower.

The strategy worked; today, we are one of the largest manufacturers of fans in the country.

'It is easy to work backwards and reduce costs and, hence, prices. But it is impossible to ask the customer to pay a higher price unless the product is of the highest quality. Most industries in India are price sensitive, especially consumer electrical. We changed the rules of the game,' says Sunil Sikka, who joined us in 2000 from Bajaj Electricals to suggest diversification into newer businesses. He would remember the lessons he learnt from QRG all his life.

Let me tell you in QRG's words why he did what he did.

'My hunch was that having a clutch of products in the same segment at hugely divergent price ranges meant that the cheaper fans would cannibalize the more expensive ones. It also implied that we had to outsource the cheaper products to small-scale units in order to reduce costs and prices; but that meant that we did not have much control over the quality of the products. So, I decided to make all the products in our factories and price them at a premium. To be successful, one has to own plants to control quality.

'At a broader level, my conviction was that companies and brands survive because of the awe and respect they generate in customers largely because of their quality. Godrej is Godrej. After 100 years of existence, no one says Godrej is a bad company. The products of Hindustan Unilever are always admired. My goal was to be known like them as a quality player. Reputation and image positioning was more important to me than revenues and profits.

'Soon, many of our products had the largest market share, commanded the highest prices, and were known for quality. Dhirubhai did the same with Vimal, which was of high quality and high price, but he also beat the competitors in terms of volumes.'

Sikka would reminisce about those hectic but enjoyable days, 'We tried to position the fans with varying USPs. For example, for possibly the first time, we talked about how our fans were better in quality; they helped the consumer conserve energy too. We introduced fans with metallic finish for the first time. We launched, what are now called, decorative fans.'

We invested decent sums of money on branding and advertising in order to expand the distribution network. Although the amounts may feel like small change compared to our current expenditure under these heads, they were mind-altering in those days for us.

To encourage the trade, and get their commitment, QRG called the dealers to Delhi during the first year of the launch. He knew that most dealers sold several brands; they had to be encouraged to push Havells. He announced special incentives for dealers who reached a certain target.

Another tactic to get the dealers on our side was our focus on after-sales service. Until then, no company offered this to the consumers as they did not feel it was important.

We felt we could develop after-sales services as a tool to gain competitive advantage for Havells fans. We built an infrastructure through franchises across the country. A dedicated call centre of thirty-six people, who could speak eight languages, was set up. We aimed to address complaints within twenty-four to forty-eight hours.

Because of our quality, there were few complaints, but we still thought this would prove useful. It paid off. The trade loved it. Most dealers hate handling angry customers; it is a waste of time and eats into their business. They were happy that Havells took on this responsibility.

Obviously, the perception and image of Havells soared in the marketplace, both among the consumers and within the trade circles. The dealers were glad to push our brand; in fact, although our advertising expenses went up, most of the publicity was through word of mouth by the dealers.

We had thought of another line of business at that time—compact fluorescent lamps, or CFLs. These were again a next-generation product. Compared to traditional incandescent lamps, CFLs used one-third to one-fifth of the power and lasted up to fifteen times longer. People had started evolving from high-energy lamps and tube lights to CFLs. As always, QRG set up a team to understand the possibilities and draw up an entry plan.

In March 2003, QRG asked how much time it would take to set up a plant to make CFLs. Before anybody else could figure that out, QRG said that he wanted it to be up and running in six months—by Diwali.

Sikka, who was in charge of the project, said that the delivery time for any equipment would be at least twelve months. QRG advised him to look for existing plants all over the world, and if a new one was available for sale, we should buy it and ship it to India. Sikka was able to locate one such plant in South Korea. Though he had visited the site a few times, for the final agreement he requested QRG to send either Ameet or me with him.

QRG told Sikka that he had complete faith in his abilities. This multiplied Sikka's confidence, and at the same time, he knew he had to be more careful about the whole deal. This is how QRG worked. Just by looking at people he would know what was going on in their minds.

QRG was not really a stranger to the lighting business. In the seventies, he had formed a relationship with an outfit called Friends & Co., a company that used to make lighting fixtures under the Havells brand. This arrangement carried on for two or three years, but didn't work out too well. So, QRG called off the partnership. But the brief engagement served its purpose—QRG got a fair idea of how the lighting business worked.

The blueprint for CFLs was ready but we wanted it to go hand in hand with fixtures (the casing that holds the lamp); we knew that lighting and fixtures were actually one business. That is how we believed the consumer saw it, and that is how we should see it as well. The consumer truly is king in our scheme of things. It was a strategic decision to become a fully fledged lighting company—a one–stop shop to meet all the demands of the buyers.

Unfortunately, fixtures were reserved for the small-scale sector. This was a vestige of the past when it was thought prudent to offer protection to small businesses. On the flip side, it created a vested interest among these businesses to stay small. The protection also bred inefficiency. Anyway, most large players got round the rules by tying up with small-scale units.

We knew it was important to make fixtures but had no option but to collaborate with a small unit. At the same time, we did not want to source from several companies; instead, we wanted to do business with one so that we could monitor the quality. Sikka was able to locate one company, called G.S. Lighting, in Gurgaon. The quality of its products was good and it was selling under its own brand, Pole Star.

G.S. Lighting was owned and run by two brothers, Krishan and Shyam Mehta. When we met them, QRG said in plain terms that he wanted to treat their factory as his own. If it required taking a minority stake in their company, QRG was prepared for it. In return, G.S. Lighting would have to become an exclusive supplier to Havells.

The Mehta brothers were agreeable to the offer but were apprehensive about one factor—their brand. They had invested time and money to build it; if they became our exclusive supplier, Pole Star would die an untimely death. They didn't want to see that happen. QRG offered to buy Pole Star from them. This clinched the deal.

Very soon, we bought a 25 per cent stake in G.S. Lighting—anything higher would have disqualified the company from being a small-scale unit—for about Rs 3 crore. We also paid the brothers Rs 1 crore for Pole Star. Meanwhile, we had set up our CFL production line inside the Faridabad factory. Havells was now also a lighting and fixtures company.

For a moment, it seemed the time was not quite right to be a domestic manufacturer of CFLs since the market was inundated with cheap imports from China. We were among the first two or three players to set up a factory. Naysayers had begun to write us off. The issue was brought to the notice of the government. The imports were causing serious injury to the domestic makers of CFLs. Soon, fortune swung our way as the government imposed an anti-dumping duty on Chinese CFLs. We were back in the game with an added advantage.

Philips had based its strategy on outsourcing the product from China and therefore it suffered a bit. Others like Indo-Asian and Orpat followed us and set up factories in India, but we had the first-mover advantage. CFL became an instant hit with the consumers. Although we did not have the distribution network for this retail (or mass) product, we asked our switchgear dealers to stock it, and they did it readily.

In 2010, lighting fixtures were taken out of the list of products reserved for the small-scale sector. It finally dawned on the government that the policy of reservations had outlived its utility. Now that cheap imports from not just China but also Vietnam and Thailand had flooded the Indian market, the small-scale sector's inefficiency had been fully exposed. It was in early 2015 that the list was completely scrapped.

With this, our arrangement with G.S. Lighting did not make sense any longer. When we set up our own factory for fixtures, the brothers wanted their brand back. We weighed our options—we had branded our fixtures as Havells Pole Star for about a year but we transited to Havells because it was a much bigger brand. Pole Star didn't hold much attraction for us. We sold the 25 per cent stake we owned in their company as well as the brand, Pole Star, back to them in 2010.

G.S. Lighting and Pole Star were an opportunity that came our way—like the T-Series fan factory—and we made full use of it. This was the hallmark of QRG's career. He had the uncanny ability to spot opportunities and then he would leverage them to the maximum extent possible.

We selected Neemrana, an industrial zone in Rajasthan (it is located near the highway that connects Delhi and

Jaipur) for our light and fixtures plant. We set up a plant of 1,00,000 square feet. Later, it occurred to us that the ceiling was low and the plant couldn't be expanded. While most others said we would have to live with it, QRG couldn't stomach it—grandeur was important for him. He said we should relocate the plant to another plot we owned.

Many remonstrated that we had already sunk close to Rs 50 crore in the plant and relocating it would burn a hole of another Rs 3 crore in our pocket. QRG asked them a simple question—what is good for the long term? The option suggested by him, they answered. That settled the matter. We moved the plant to a bigger plot—this time with a higher ceiling.

QRG built factories the way people build houses—with a twenty-five-year perspective. Most other companies don't look beyond a ten–year horizon. That's why we always hired the best architects, like C.P. Kukreja Associates, for our factories, even though we knew that they were the most expensive. *'Jahan satyanash,'* QRG liked to say, *'Wahan sava satyanash.'* If you are going in, you should go in all the way. That's why our factories look more like information technology centres than traditional plants.

The first decade of this century was also the time we upscaled and consolidated our manufacturing operations. The factory at Alwar has expanded from five acres to 100 acres. We bought adjacent plots, largely in auctions held by RIICO. One plot was across the road from our factory. Once, when Rajasthan Chief Minister Vasundhara Raje had come to inaugurate the midday meal scheme we started for children at Alwar, I told her about this problem and how it was impacting operations. Very kindly, she agreed to divert the road so that we could consolidate our operations.

We decided to house all production of domestic switchgear at our unit in Baddi in Himachal Pradesh, a tax–concession zone. We decided to make industrial switchgear at Faridabad and Sahibabad (the old Towers & Transformers factory). All production of Standard was moved to Haridwar in Uttarakhand, another tax-concession zone. The Jalandhar land is still with us. Finally, at Neemrana, we set up a huge complex to make motors, pumps, CFLs and water-storage heaters (or geysers—more on that later), apart from lighting and fixtures.

Most of these investments were funded out of internal accruals and debt. Since we were not very profitable till 2002–03, there was always a sizeable debt on Havells's books. But we were careful that interest outgo did not strangulate our cash flows and restrict our operations.

One reason for the debt was that our equity base was small. Somehow, the equity market was cold to us. Our products had done well in the market, we had absorbed smaller companies and had found foreign partners—all of that did not cut much ice with the investors. As a result, since 1993, we had not been able to raise our equity capital. It was too small for a company of our size.

And as the market for mergers and acquisitions was heating up, we realized that a larger equity base could give us vital acquisition currency. In many big-ticket deals, the buyers offered some payment, or even the whole payment, in stock. We didn't want to be hamstrung by inadequate capital, more so because we were now fully in 'growth through acquisition' mode. Equity compliments debt when it comes to investments. The two need to go hand in hand. In our case, there was too much reliance on debt, which was not ideal.

But we were conscious that the market was indifferent towards us, and our shares recorded very low volumes. One reason was that we did not communicate frequently with the investor community—either directly or through the media.

We knew that we were grossly undervalued. Our share price did not reflect the intrinsic value of our business. We had to address this problem.

In 2002–03, Rajesh Gupta, the CFO, and I began doing the rounds of fund managers and investment analysts in Mumbai. It was then that reality hit us—they took a very dim view of companies based out of Delhi. It was a serious perception problem.

We had gone to meet Prashant Jain, the chief investment officer of HDFC. As soon as we showed him our financial, he asked us bluntly, 'Are these profits real?' We were very hurt, and it probably showed on our faces. Jain then narrated his bitter experiences with Delhi companies. Many had shown him fake assets and books. Some wouldn't agree to factory visits. It must have been a harrowing experience for him.

This was akin to what Guruji had told QRG many years ago. We understood his concern but felt that there was no need to tar everybody with the same brush. The solution was to get a well-known private equity fund to invest in us, which would have been a big vote of confidence.

Two of them, ChrysCapital and CLSA, showed interest in Havells. Finally, in late 2004, CLSA bought around

7 per cent in the company for $5 million, valuing it at Rs 300 crore, which was way above the then market capitalization of Havells. Our first objective was achieved.

In a few short months, by January 2005, other funds too had developed an appetite for Havells stock. QRG was also allured. We decided to raise another Rs 80 crore, which we thought would help us bankroll some acquisition. Citi and ChrysCapital were the front runners this time. Each wanted to invest $20 million in us.

But fate had something else in store. Sometime in 2004, Standard Chartered had taken a few Indian corporate leaders on a tour of China. Among those invited were Ashish Bharatram of SRF, then Wipro CFO Suresh Senapathy, Gautam Thapar of Ballarpur Industries and Infosys honcho T.V. Mohandas Pai. As luck would have it, I too was invited to be a part of this delegation. Needless to say, I was elated, especially because all the invited companies were much bigger than us. During the trip, I struck up a warm relationship with Bharatram and Mohandas Pai.

In fact, our midday meal programme at Alwar was started at Mohandas Pai's behest. On one visit to Bangalore, I met him and told him about the private equity deal we were planning to close soon. He asked me if we needed money urgently. When I said no, Mohandas Pai said we shouldn't raise money now—we should wait till the valuation of the company improves. His logic was simple, the first infusion by CLSA was done with a purpose of generating confidence among the investor community. The next fund raise should only be done when funds were actually needed.

His suggestion made a lot of sense to me. I too began to wonder why we should sell Havells's equity cheap. I immediately called QRG from Bangalore and told him about it. He also saw the logic. We said no to both Citi and ChrysCapital. Ashish Dhawan, who headed ChrysCapital at that time, called up Mohandas Pai in Bangalore and asked him to persuade us to do the deal. Perhaps he knew that we were close. But we stood our ground. Of course, it proved to be the right decision.

The investor apathy of those financial years did not mean that we were blind to financial innovation. In fact, the nineties and the noughties were the decades when we created unique financial products, which made Havells almost cash-proof, or rather free from fears of cash squeezes in the normal business environment. Our flow of cash became so smooth that we did not even have to discuss it. Only in exceptional cases, did this become a matter of concern.

One of the first ones on the anvil was buyers' credit in the mid-nineties, when we entered the cables and wires categories. This was a strange business, where no supplier of raw materials gave any credit; payments to them had to be made instantly. However, the buyers of Havells's wires and cables demanded a credit period, and wanted to pay after a few months.

It created a total mismatch between our expenses and revenues. While the former had to be paid immediately, the returns from sales came after a few months. In case the latter got stuck because of a slight change in market conditions, the cash flows worsened. It was a classical cash trap.

There would be daily fights between the finance department and the production division; the latter wanted to buy raw materials faster to boost production, and the former wanted to stabilize the purchases to strike a balance between cash spent and cash earned. The manufacturing wing blamed finance for slower sales growth; finance blamed manufacturing for cash mismanagement.

With the help of HDFC Bank, we were able to resolve the issue. Havells would buy the raw materials, and HDFC Bank would immediately pay the suppliers. In addition, HDFC Bank would extend a credit period of ninety days to us to repay the money. To de-risk HDFC Bank, we gave them post-dated cheques for the amounts paid to the suppliers.

We were convinced we had sorted out all our financial management issues until we met Bharat Shah of ASK Raymond James, an analysts firm, along with other institutional investors in 2002. Shah was one of the few who asked us several questions, and one of them stumped us. A decade after being listed on the Indian stock exchanges, no one had even hinted we had a problem on this front.

Shah's query was simple, yet intriguing—where is the 'colour of money'? Initially, we had no clue what he meant or what he referred to. We were told that Shah's complaint was that our businesses had negative cash flows in the past decade. In other words, the cash generated in the business was unable to meet our expenses, and our fast growth was being funded by increasing working capital debt. And the analyst saw no efforts on our part to make it positive. He said this could not continue.

The question propelled Havells to undertake an innovative financial re-engineering, one which no other

Indian company had done before. The only way to get into positive cash flow was to reduce the loans on our balance sheet, especially the working capital loans. However, given the nature of our business, it was almost impossible to achieve this objective.

It took us five to six months to evolve a financial product, which was a mix of insurance and banking. Apart from Havells, three parties were involved in this slightly complex product, which included our dealers, suppliers, bankers and insurance companies.

Thus, our sales invoices, which we issued to the distributors and dealers who purchased our products, were sold to the banks in cash. These invoices were backed by insurance and, therefore, the banks were assured that they would not lose any money even if we did not get the payments. We could now use the cash to pay the suppliers in time and take advantage of early payments.

Most of our balance sheet problems were solved because of this innovation. First, as Shah had desired, we became cash-flow positive because the working-capital loans that we took to spend money while we waited for buyers to pay us, vanished from the balance sheet.

Second, since our sales invoices were cashable immediately, or could be converted into cash, we were in a position to spend efficiently and keep our suppliers happy. No vendor has had an issue in over a decade about his payments being delayed.

Finally, the insurance-banking product excited our distributors and dealers. Now that we got revenues from sales almost instantly from the banks, we had the option to increase the credit period to the buyers. In fact, we doubled the credit period for dealers from forty-five to ninety days, which helped us expand our business.

All this time, the only cloud on the horizon was QRG's health. After the first tryst with sepsis in late 2001, he had to be treated for major infections at hospitals during the winter months over the next three years. It weakened him physically to quite an extent but his faculties were as sharp as before. Due to rheumatoid arthritis and interstitial lung disease, QRG was perpetually on steroids, which gave him severe osteoporosis. Osteoporosis is a condition when bones in the body become weak due to lack of calcium.

On 1 January 2006, QRG fractured his backbone, not due to an injury, but due to osteoporosis. For the first few days, we lost hope of him ever standing on his feet again. Worst of all, he also lost hope. For the first time, he was depressed and had started losing interest in any business discussion that I would bring home to him. He would simply look the other way. No medicine was effective and doctors also gave him a very slim chance of recovery.

However, after a few days, QRG started gaining confidence, and resolved that even if it took a few months, he would not lose hope. However, it was not before June that he could finally stand up. He resumed work in July, though he had to wear a full brace for the rest of his life. I remember that when he came to the office and addressed all the senior heads of branches at a half-yearly meeting, nobody could sense that he had been bedridden for as long as six months. It was during these days that he talked to all his family members and senior executives and made me the joint managing director of the company.

In December 2007, he had sepsis once again and was in the hospital for three weeks. But the show must go on, he would say. QRG used to participate in teleconferences from his room in the hospital. That wasn't all—he had a major bypass surgery in 2008. A lot of people had written him off then. He came back and won the biggest battle of his life—and our lives.

FIFTEEN

The Sylvania Files

Success begets confidence. And by the middle of the noughties, our confidence was sky high. In 2005, our annual turnover was almost Rs 700 crore with net profits of Rs 30 crore. Within a decade, our revenues had multiplied almost seven times from Rs 100 crore. Clearly, we were on a vertical growth curve. Havells was seen as a mid-sized group, which had the potential to enter the big league and compete effectively with the likes of Philips and Siemens. We were the young Turks of India Inc.

There was a lot of energy flowing through Havells that needed an outlet. Many people within the organization had started seeking new challenges. We had entered new lines of business and had done rather well for ourselves. We had completed the Standard Electricals acquisition successfully. People were wondering what our next move would be.

During that decade, India Inc. itself had undergone a huge transformation. Several Indian groups, like the ones led by Ratan Tata and Kumar Mangalam Birla, had come to be known as Indian multinational corporations. They had acquired large companies abroad; they had proved that Indians were soon going to become key players in the global arena. Everyone talked about the emergence of globalized Indian players.

Apart from the large business houses, companies like Ranbaxy, SRF, Dabur, Sona Steering, Samtel, Dr Reddy's Laboratories and others were also picking up international assets.

Saikat Chaudhuri, then a management professor at Wharton University, said towards the end of 2006, 'Over the last decade, Indian firms in various industries—most visibly in information technology but also in areas like auto components, the energy sector and food products— have been slowly building up to become emerging multinationals.' He added that in the years to come, Indian companies would 'seek out acquisitions that help them move up the value chain'.

A study by the New Delhi-based Institute for Studies in Industrial Development quoted analysis which said that the overseas acquisitions by Indian firms 'possessed three objectives—access to international market, acquiring firm-specific created assets, and benefits from operating synergies with overseas targets'. Therefore, the ISID study concluded that overseas acquisitions by Indian multinationals 'have been directed with a set of multifaceted firm-specific objectives'.

That was also the time when businessmen felt that growth opportunities lay outside India. The India-centred growth story happened much later. That's why companies across sectors—automotive, pharmaceuticals, FMCG, energy, etc. made aggressive acquisitions abroad.

Going by the statistics, Indian firms spent just over $2.5 billion to take over twenty-one firms in 2002; the figures for 2005 were over $3.5 billion to acquire 135 overseas firms, and nearly $7.7 billion to buy out 177 international companies in 2006. In 2007, India Inc. spent almost $40 billion on overseas buys—a huge jump by any standard.

Some of the high-profile Indian buyouts that happened in the 2005–07 period included the spectacular purchase of the UK's Corus Steel by Tata Steel, aluminium manufacturer Hindalco's takeover of Novellis in the US, state-owned ONGC Videsh's acquisitions in Sudan, Brazil, Russia and Angola, and Videocon's buyout of Thomson's cathode ray tube division. (Tata Motors's purchase of Jaguar Land Rover would happen later.)

In a growing number of cross-border deals, names of Indian buyers began to crop up. Indian managers could make do with fewer resources and still produce great results. This, it was believed, gave Indian managers the capability to trim bloated western companies and turn them around. Indians deal with different cultures at the workplace and can generally speak three languages efficiently, English being one of them. This gave Indian companies a distinct advantage in managing global operations.

One particular acquisition that had caught our attention was Tata Tea's purchase of Tetley in 2000. At £271 million, it was the largest overseas acquisition by an Indian company at that time. Tetley, the 160-year-old British company and the inventor of the teabag, was almost twice the size of Tata Tea, yet the Indian company had bought it. Had Tata Tea gone abroad on its own, it would have taken years, if not decades, to get a global footprint.

This purchase helped it reduce the go-to-market time—it catapulted Tata Tea straight away into the big league.

What also got us interested in the deal was the way it was structured. Tata Tea had bought it from Schroder Ventures and PPM Ventures (they had acquired it from Allied Domecq through a management buyout) through a leveraged buyout. What it meant was that the acquisition was funded from debt raised on the balance sheet of the acquired company, and the debt, and the interest on it, would be paid out of the cash generated by it.

We liked this concept. Such an acquisition would give us geographical reach without straining the balance sheet of Havells too much. And, if required, we could always raise equity. Mohandas Pai's advice that we shouldn't keep cash in the company unless we needed it had served us well—with each quarter, our valuation was improving.

The biggest proponent of the overseas thrust was QRG, who was now approaching seventy while battling his poor health. Yet, the thrill of stepping into untested waters hadn't left him. Though we were all on the same page, QRG was the driving force behind this. Nine out of ten people would have been satisfied to hang up their boots after what he had achieved—it was indeed a long distance he had covered from Malerkotla. But there were no full stops for QRG. 'What next?' he would always ask, spurring us on.

The first opportunity for us to go abroad had come in 2005 when Geyer offered its Greek company, where it used to make MCBs, to us. As I mentioned earlier, we had collaborated with Geyer, of Germany, many years ago. After Albert Geyer's death, the business went into decline. Finally, the Greek unit was put on the block.

In a limited way, we were attracted to the unit. There were several reasons for this. First, the acquisition, although small, would give us access to south and south-east markets in Europe. We thought it would help us sell MCBs in Germany, a large and thriving market. Second, it would offer an opportunity to get European quality certification in switchgears. Finally, there was synergy since 40 per cent of our exports in 2005 were to Europe.

But after a month of due diligence, we realized that the company had become too weak over the years, though the acquisition would have cost us close to nothing. Its sales were small, and its presence in Germany was negligible. It would have brought us no strategic advantage. So, we opted out of the race. Later, we came to learn, the unit went into liquidation.

But the whole exercise did serve some purpose. It gave us insights into the intricate, tricky and sensitive discussions that are part of any overseas deal.

Around the same time as we grappled with the Greek company, we got another thrilling opportunity.

As I mentioned earlier, we had an excellent relationship with Electrium, the new avatar of Hanson Electricals after it was acquired by its CEO, Chris Thomas, in a management buyout. In 2005, when the private equity shareholders decided to exit Electrium and pocket their returns on their original investments, Thomas asked us if we were interested in it. He told us that we could bid for Electrium if we wished to.

QRG agreed immediately. He, like all of us, had been interested in a large international acquisition that could catapult Havells on to the global stage.

Electrium's annual turnover at that stage was £80 million and it made profits of low double digits, so we estimated that the sale price would be around £60–70 million. It seemed reasonable. We also negotiated with the existing management team that they would continue to run the company and retain a minority stake. We had a lot of confidence in our relationship with them. Even in 2005, our Electrium-related business, including the products sold in India and the UK, was worth Rs 60–70 crore a year.

However, other players were interested in the company and before we knew it, there was an auction to contend with. More importantly, we had to fight against global giants like Siemens and Schneider to wrest control of Electrium. It took us little time to realize that our bid had to be much higher than the earlier estimate of £60–70 million. The new price in our minds was £80 million.

Although most of us were worried about the higher price, QRG urged us to go ahead. For him, a few million pounds here and there did not matter. He seemed focused on the fact that Electrium was the right fit, and that extra revenues could be earned through hard work and strategic changes.

We got Deutsche Bank to underwrite the potential purchase price. We had known Gunit Chaddha, the head of Deutsche Bank in India, from his days at IDBI Bank.

When the bids were opened, we realized we had been heavily outbid. We heard that Siemens had made the highest offer of just under £100 million. We felt that Siemens was overpaying for the company and decided not to raise our bid. The company was then acquired by Siemens.

We lost Electrium but decided to wait for another takeover opportunity.

The opportunity came a year later, in November 2006. Rajesh Gupta, our CFO, had attended a bankers' conclave in South Africa where he had met representatives from Rothschild, the famous investment bank. During their talks, he told the Rothschild representative, Naveen Wadhwani, that Havells was looking for an overseas acquisition.

Later, Wadhwani came to know that Rothschild's New York office had got the mandate to sell Sylvania, the lighting company. For some strange reason, Sylvania was not offered to buyers in China and India but he contacted us immediately.

The proposal was quite straightforward. Sylvania had a turnover of almost €500 million and an operational profit of around €30 million. The owners were looking at a price-earnings multiple of seven. So, for around €200 million, the company could be ours. Also, since we were interested in a leveraged buyout, we were told that Sylvania had the capacity to mobilize up to €140 million of debt. In other words, with an investment of €60 million from Havells, we could potentially buy out Sylvania.

Of course, we were instantly interested.

Sylvania had an illustrious past. It had started life as Hygrade Sylvania in 1931 in the United States. In 1939, it made the world's first tubular fluorescent lamp, or tube light. In 1959, it merged with General Telephones to form General Telephones & Electronics. This company, in 1993, decided to sell the Sylvania lighting business to Osram of Germany.

Sylvania was strong in both Europe and the Americas. When Osram was set to acquire it, the European

Commission said it would lead to a monopoly in Europe. Osram was actually only interested in the American business of Sylvania. So, it acquired the American business, which comprised the United States, Canada and Mexico, while the rest was sold to Citi Ventures Capital.

Sylvania then went through bankruptcy and was purchased by a clutch of private equity funds—DDJ Capital, Cerberus Capital Management and JP Morgan—which turned it around in due course. And now they had put it on the block. Being financial investors, they felt it was time for them to book profits on their investments.

There was a reason why QRG was interested in this company. Sylvania had a presence in India through a company called Sylvania & Laxman that was set up in 1962. Its factory was located at Najafgarh Road, not far from Kirti Nagar where Havells had set up its first unit in the seventies. In the seventies and eighties, its products were doing quite well in the market. QRG remembered that Sylvania Laxman was an even bigger brand than Philips in India. In the last few years, the business had gone into decline but there was no denying Sylvania's brand equity.

At that time, the worldwide electrical market was around $1 trillion in value but was highly fragmented. Average profitability, various studies suggested, was in the range of 5–8 per cent. Most markets were growing at the same rate as their GDP. The United States was, of course, the largest market with a share of 29 per cent. Western Europe, comprising sixteen countries, came second with a share of 22 per cent—China and India had not exploded on the world scene then.

QRG was clear that our next phase of growth would come from the acquisition of a strong company in the West. Sylvania fit the bill perfectly. I was in total agreement.

Some people had their doubts despite QRG's enthusiasm. We had entered the lighting business in India a few years ago, and we did not know much about the domestic business, let alone the global market. Was it a good idea to take over one of the top four lighting companies in the world? Also, wouldn't it be wiser for us to grow in switchgear, which was highly profitable rather than lighting?

Switchgear, obviously, was a better fit than lighting, but the fact was that the bigwigs like Schneider, Siemens and ABB, had started gobbling up mid-sized switchgear companies, which left very few opportunities for people like us.

There were other issues as well. Unlike Electrium, where we knew the company as well as its management, our information about Sylvania was sketchy, to say the least. Was it a good idea to walk into unknown territory? Our well-wishers advised us to be cautious.

Sylvania was one and a half times bigger than us in terms of revenues. We had very little experience in global markets, except for our exports and the aborted acquisition of Electrium. Did we have the expertise, skill and management bandwidth to deal with Sylvania managerially, operationally and technologically, they asked. Were we about to bite off more than we could chew?

Clearly, Sylvania would be a much larger acquisition than Electrium in terms of its price tag. It was twice as expensive, or even more. We had the ability to raise the money required for the purchase but did we have the fortitude to manage such a huge expenditure?

These were all valid issues. A risk-averse person might have even given up this quest, but no dream was too big for QRG.

As the naysayers debated the matter, QRG's enthusiasm had already set the acquisition ball in motion. Rothschild was told we were interested. Internally, Ameet, Sikka and Rajesh Gupta were asked to pore over Sylvania's balance sheets and other documents that were available in the public domain. Sylvania was definitely on our radar.

The negotiations immediately hit a roadblock. Rothschild said that our offer would come into play only if the existing bidder on the table was rejected by Sylvania. Though we could not learn the identity of the bidder, we immediately had visions of the Electrium fiasco. We feared having to go down the auction route again where we risked overpaying; we may have been ambitious, but we were not reckless.

QRG felt the same way. We had to act fast and decisively. Encouraged by QRG's infectious aggression and enthusiasm, I too got excited by Sylvania.

The shareholders of Sylvania (it was closely held) had mandated the company's CEO, Paul Griswold, to find a buyer, negotiate and sell the company.

I called up Griswold and told him that we were in the lighting business and, hence, we were a serious buyer. I questioned why he was looking to sell Sylvania to pure-play financial investors, who would invariably rip the company apart, sell off its various assets and ruin it. In contrast, we would run the company as it was, for we were in the business for the long haul.

Griswold maintained that the current discussions were in late stages, and it would take time to allow a new bidder into the fray as it would involve fresh discussions with the board and lawyers. I did not give up; I asked him if we could meet on Monday (this discussion happened on Friday).

Reluctantly, he agreed to meet us on Tuesday. Our team flew to New York right away. There was no time to lose.

That was our first meeting with Griswold. Then in his fifties, he was a mountain of a man—six feet, eight inches tall, and weighing 125 kg. He had an impressive bearing and was a convincing talker. We had nobody like him in our team. In very little time, we were under his spell.

While Griswold told us about the company, we made a presentation on our plans vis-à-vis Sylvania and Havells, and put in a bid for €200 million. Deutsche Bank agreed to underwrite the purchase price, as it had done with Electrium.

Suddenly, during the first week of December 2006, things became eerily quiet. Despite repeated calls, we got no replies from either Sylvania or its investors. We were piqued but decided to relax and not worry. We disengaged ourselves from the deal for a few days.

Fortunately, Sylvania came back to us and the deal was back on track. However, the company said that while we could start the due diligence process, it would not give us 'exclusivity' which meant that others could also bid at a later stage. We insisted on exclusivity as we did not want a bidding war, or an auction, after our experience with Electrium. We wanted to wrap up this deal as quickly as possible.

I tried another tactic; I proposed a meeting between Sylvania's shareholders and Havells's team to thrash out pending issues, including the price. It was mutually agreed to hold the meeting on 15 December. The place chosen was a resort at Chantilly, near Sylvania's main European warehouse in Paris. There were three of us—Ameet, Sikka and me. On their side, Griswold had come with Jackson Craig, the main shareholder of DDJ Capital.

At this meeting, Craig led the discussions. He was short, sharp, financially savvy and to the point. Our discussion moved back and forth during the day. Finally, we broke up for dinner. It was just the four of us—Griswold, Craig, Ameet and me. Craig came to the point straightaway and said we needed to offer more. I told him that we could raise our offer to €225 million. Craig demanded €230 million but finally settled for €227.5 million. We shook hands over that.

Immediately, I sent an SMS to Apurva Shah of Deutsche Bank, who was having dinner with other Sylvania executives at another restaurant. He messaged me back, 'Let's wait till tomorrow.' Often, for some inexplicable reason, investment bankers develop cold feet at the last moment, especially if it's a big-ticket deal. But that's not how entrepreneurs work. I sent him back another message, 'Already done.' That was it.

Over the next few weeks, Ernst & Young did a quick due diligence of Sylvania, and concluded that the price we had offered was slightly high—about €10–15 million—since the company's profitability was weak. QRG felt the price differential between the fair price and our bid was too low and, if this was the only risk, it was not an important one.

In fact, during the 15 December meeting, when the bid was finalized, QRG was in constant touch with both Ameet and me to find out about the deal. He pushed us to close the deal the same day, and questioned why we were unable to do so. Ameet later quipped that he found it difficult to deal with the seller's queries and QRG's questions almost at the same time!

By February 2007, a few more adjustments were made to the contractual clauses. Finally, the agreement was ready to be signed in March. One day before the Havells board was supposed to meet, at Hotel Imperial in downtown New Delhi, Craig said he hadn't read the documents fully and needed more time. This sent us into a tizzy—we had not just called the board meeting but had also told the media that we were going to make a big announcement. I called up Craig right away but he wouldn't budge. We had to reschedule our plans, which was not easy.

The deal was finally completed ten days later, and we made the payments in April 2007. We had Sylvania—we were ecstatic. We had arrived on the global scene.

SIXTEEN

CEO Has to Go

The Sylvania deal was financially very well crafted. We raised a debt of €120 million on Sylvania's balance sheet, with no guarantee of any kind from Havells, and another €80 million on Havells's balance sheet.

Even before we signed the deal, several private equity funds wanted to invest in us. Two of them had shown a particularly high level of interest—Citibank and Warburg Pincus. We told them that we would contact them whenever we needed the funds. Once the Sylvania acquisition was done, we placed 11 per cent equity in Havells with Warburg Pincus for $110 million, which was equivalent to €80 million. With this money, the company paid off the banks and became debt-free once again.

That, as it turned out, was the easier part of the deal.

Cross-border acquisitions, especially when a company from an emerging market like India acquires a global giant in a developed nation, are often hyped and exaggerated.

The foremost reason is that of disbelief—how can a puny and unknown firm purchase a renowned name? The second is the huge amounts, mostly in hundreds of millions of dollars, paid by the acquirer. The third is the expectation of the formation of a new joint entity, whose combined synergies could easily result in higher revenues and profits. One plus one in such cases adds up to three or even five!

However, the failure rate in acquisitions, both small and big, within a country and cross-border, is extremely high. Most studies done by McKinsey and other think tanks have concluded that the figure could be as high as 50 per cent. The commonly cited reasons for the post-acquisition blues include over-inflated price, poor strategic fit, failure to leverage synergies, and changes in market conditions.

What is normally forgotten in such discussions is that one of the foremost reasons for acquisitions not being able to capture the underlying values is related to corporate cultures. McKinsey surveys over the years have revealed that a majority of corporate managers believe that a lack of 'culture fit' between the acquirer and target companies results in an imminent fiasco.

Susan Cartwright argues that mergers and acquisitions are 'rarely a marriage of equals and it's still the case that most acquirers or dominant merger partners pursue a strategy of cultural absorption . . . the unfortunate part is that few organizations bother to understand the cultural values . . . of their merging partners . . .'

According to McKinsey, '80 per cent (of the managers polled in a survey) admitted that culture is hard to define. Therein lays the rub. How can you address cultural problems, if you don't know what you're trying to fix? Hardly surprising then, that most executives feel more comfortable dealing with costs and synergies than culture, despite the potential of culture to enhance or destroy merger value.'

Therefore, many promoters take the easy way out. They keep the acquirer and target companies apart for several years until they recognize how to unleash the combined synergies after a cultural amalgamation. This is especially true when a smaller company takes over a larger one.

In our case, the situation was more complex. As I have mentioned, we had little experience in the lighting business, and about the global market. Thus, the intricacies of Sylvania's production, marketing and technology were a bit hazy to us.

Once the takeover was in its final stages, we sought out people who had done overseas acquisitions to learn from them how to manage businesses at remote destinations. As we didn't know Ratan Tata or Kumar Mangalam Birla, we decided to contact others. We sought the advice of Mohandas Pai, Akhil Gupta of Bharti Airtel and Arvind Dham of Amtek Auto, a Delhi-based maker of automobile components.

We didn't know Dham. But through an acquaintance, we sought a meeting with him at his office in south Delhi. He met us warmly and said something that was so true. 'So long as you have not signed on the dotted line, your investment banker will be by your side, you will stay in good hotels and travel in good cars,' he told QRG and me. 'Once the deal is done and you need to go to the factory, you will be all alone.' The message was—you cannot run an overseas business with remote control. We would soon learn this the hard way.

Havells's buyout of Sylvania was a case of David taking over Goliath; so, we were unsure if we could impose our business philosophy or culture on the latter. More importantly, we didn't have any experience in managing a global business, with employees and other stakeholders based in dozens of nations, which had inherited global best practices over decades.

The fact remains that Sylvania's annual turnover then was around €500 million, it had dozens of factories strewn across several continents, it was a very old brand, its products were sold in fifty countries, and its marketing network included 10,000 distributors and dealers.

When we took over Sylvania, its operations were spread out, largely across Europe and South America. We had no knowledge about the laws and business environment in many of these countries. We were saddled with a negative mindset, filled with insecurities and apprehensions. These fears were not about the takeover, but our ability to run Sylvania. Unfortunately, we chose the easiest option; we decided to tread the road most travelled.

Not only did we decide to keep Sylvania separate from Havells, although the former's name was changed to Havells Sylvania, we retained the senior management team, including the CEO, Griswold. Post-takeover, Havells Sylvania was managed in the same manner as it was earlier. We looked only at the key operational figures on a monthly and quarterly basis.

To be fair, although QRG would strongly dispute it, I strongly advocated that there was no point in changing a stable formula. One reason was that the banks who had loaned us money for the acquisition found it very reassuring when we said that we would continue with the old management. We were soon going to find out how wrong that approach was.

The owners of Sylvania had constituted a four-member committee, which comprised CEO Griswold, the CFO, chief legal officer and chief supply chain officer. The committee ran the company from New York. Such was our faith in them that we took them on board with promises of a huge payout in case they were to exit!

Griswold had the right pedigree and experience backed by results. Most private equity funds continue with CEOs only if the latter deliver the desired goods. Griswold had done it. And we saw no pressing need to tamper with the successful formula.

According to an article in *Business Today*, he had 'turned Sylvania around after it slipped into bankruptcy in 2002 and made it profitable . . .' Why should we rock the boat? I felt that there was no need to tinker around with its management. Moreover, along with my younger colleagues, I did not wish to impose an Indian entrepreneurial philosophy on Sylvania.

Griswold was based in New York, he travelled to Europe quite frequently—the bulk of Sylvania's manufacturing operations were in Europe and South America. This was the manner in which he had operated in the past, these were the terms he finalized with the previous owners, and this was the way in which things continued. The management control of the company was essentially with Griswold.

We did not interfere with most of his decisions, though we did interact with senior managers like division or geographical heads. But since Griswold was the buffer between Sylvania and Havells, many of them did not act upon our advice.

There was no integration between Havells and Sylvania, either in terms of operations or finances (although we paid for the company), forget about cultural integration—while Havells was energetic and informal, Sylvania was staid and laid-back. If we continued with Griswold, it was because we felt safe that someone with experience and a proven record was running the show.

Thus, after we had acquired Sylvania, we called the top sixty executives for a meeting. It was held in an office we had recently rented in Noida. We also took them on a chartered aircraft to Baddi to show them our factory.

At that time, Havells was focused on growth. All our discussions would revolve around how to bump up growth. This became the centrepiece of our interaction with the Sylvania managers. We thought we would infuse them with energy and that would take care of everything else. There was no talk of improving efficiencies and becoming leaner. We didn't feel the need for it.

Sylvania's top management lived in New York, flew to Europe every Monday, and was back in New York on Thursday evening. It was management at arm's length and we acted like investors. The CEO gave us the budgets and growth figures, and we evaluated them regularly. We thought that the system would gradually work; we did not press for changes in the decision-making process.

We had no emotional connect with the employees. We felt that the European way of doing business was different. It worked for a while as the global markets remained healthy in 2007.

But it turned out to be a huge mistake on our part. The consequences of the hands-off approach were dire, to say the least. When the global financial crisis of 2008 (that had begun to rear its head towards the latter half of 2007) occurred, the mistake quickly turned into a disaster.

This crisis was initially dubbed as the Second Great Depression and was expected to convulse the global economy into a decade-long depression similar to the one that had taken place in the thirties. Later called the Great Recession, because most economies, especially the US, came out of the trough within three to five years, it impacted the entire world, including Europe.

A research paper in September 2013 estimated that the output loss to the US economy between December 2007 and June 2009 because of the crisis was between $6 trillion and $14 trillion.

The same study found that the 'US household net worth plunged by $16 trillion, or 24 per cent, from third quarter of 2007 to first quarter of 2009'. In addition, there were 'harder-to-quantify impacts of the crisis', whose consequences included 'extended unemployment, reduced opportunity and increased government presence in the economy'. The total impact of the crisis, concluded the analysis, exceeded 'the value of the nation's output for an entire year'.

The European situation was a bit different. Its banks and financial service firms were almost wiped out by the crisis, as was the private sector in nations like Spain and Italy that had become big borrowers prior to 2008. Post-crisis, the debt situation worsened as the governments had to borrow more. Essentially, the PIIGS (Portugal, Ireland, Italy, Greece and Spain) countries faced the worst crisis.

Both the US and European Union announced huge official bailouts and economic stimuli to lift up the economies; the bailout figure for Europe was $200 billion.

Shaken by the crisis, Sylvania walked into the disaster zone. Sales fell; the bottom line had red ink all over it. In 2008–09, the net loss was over €16 million; sales fell in two consecutive years, 2008–09 and 2009–10. But the realization that things were bad hit us almost six months later.

Most importantly, we had no clue about what was wrong with the company. Though we had regular meetings with the top team in New York, we had no contact with the managers on the ground. To communicate with them, we had to go through Griswold. He was the bridge between Sylvania's management and us; he was also the funnel through which information was filtered out to us.

This was not the way we took decisions at Havells. We believed in open and transparent discussions that cut across hierarchies. In Havells, a mid-level manager could talk directly to QRG and vice versa. In many morning meetings, QRG would call a junior employee and ask him key questions about sales, inventories or the progress of the implementation of some work in a specific plant—but always in the presence of his superior. There was no possibility of mixed messages getting transmitted down the line.

We also began to realize that Griswold, apart from being expansive, was also short-tempered and did not take well to suggestions. In several conversations, whenever we made a few suggestions on how to mend things, he bluntly told us that our remedies were wrong, and this was not the way companies were managed in Europe. All our ideas, good or bad, were shot down at the CEO's level. Griswold said we did not understand the nuances of European management and he alone knew how to turn around Sylvania.

In September–October 2008, Sylvania did the unthinkable. It breached the banks' covenants; it failed to stick to the projections of financial ratios that we had promised to the lenders prior to the acquisition. In western corporate jargon, it was akin to an inability to repay loans. We were on the verge of an imminent takeover by the banks if they so insisted. It was a grave crisis.

Sylvania's buyout had been financed through a loan of €140 million, whose repayment was based on being able to adhere to pre-accepted projections of monthly and quarterly cash flows. If the company failed to achieve them, it was a breach of covenants.

More than anything else, it was a serious loss of face for us. Not only would we lose the company, we would incur losses on the purchase price. Havells's reputation was on the block, so to speak, something we could not afford. QRG was worried.

The rumours that Sylvania could take Havells down along with it spread among our dealers and distributors. The buzz was that our group was on its way to oblivion. At this stage, QRG took his first direct initiative on the Sylvania conundrum.

QRG called the Havells dealers, especially those in north India, to his office and told them that despite Sylvania's problems, Havells was in good shape. He said that there were challenges, but we would set things right. He gave them assurances that he would personally intervene to 'fix' Sylvania. They were relieved.

Meanwhile, some people had started telling us that we should sell Sylvania for €1, write off the €80 million we had invested and cut all our losses, otherwise Havells would sink too. But QRG said that if we had to lose money, we might as well try to turn around Sylvania.

From his perspective, and rightly so, QRG said that I, along with some others, had 'mismanaged' Sylvania. His comments sounded a bit harsh then as we had acted in good faith. However, I have to take the blame as I depended too much on Griswold and his team. I decided that I would get Sylvania back on track with QRG's guidance.

Before we could think about the restructuring of Sylvania, we had to tackle two key issues. The first was to create a connection with the bankers. Until now, Griswold had been the buffer between us and the lenders; we had rarely met the latter, who had been consistently briefed by the CEO. The banks were uncomfortable with us; they distrusted us and felt that we wouldn't be able to manage Sylvania. All the decisions flowed from Griswold. Thus, the bankers asked us to repay the loans immediately or, as they suggested through Griswold, we should sell the company under the banks' supervision. The third option they gave us was to sink more promoters' money, €2–3 million a month for the next year or so, into Sylvania. All the three options were either unacceptable or impractical.

As we sought ways to strike a chord with the bankers, we had to deal with Griswold. We received feedback, which was never confirmed, that the CEO saw this as a great personal opportunity. He seemed to have told the lenders that we couldn't manage Sylvania and, therefore, the banks should help him launch a management buyout of the company.

There was no way we could have continued with him on board. QRG was never in favour of firing people, however bad their performance might be, and he was clearly reluctant to ask Griswold to go. In fact, letting people go was completely against QRG's nature. He believed in giving people second chances. He felt the same way about Griswold.

However, by December 2008, I had managed to convince QRG that we had to get rid of Griswold and, if required, several other senior executives.

The question was, would we be able to manage on our own? QRG was of the view that all businesses, wherever they may be located, required similar management and entrepreneurial skills. There was little difference between managing a firm in India or London or New York. One of his favourite quotes was, '*Jo Lahore fuddu, woh sab jagah fuddu*', or one who cannot succeed in a thriving market like Lahore—one of the largest in pre-Independence India—cannot succeed anywhere else either.

Logically, in the case of Sylvania, he implied that if we could do well in India, a market with hundreds of millions of middle-class consumers, then we could do so in Europe and South America as well.

Therefore, he told me to seize management control at Sylvania. The first step in this direction was to let Griswold go. He said that employees and other stakeholders should realize that we were in charge of Sylvania, and not Griswold and his select team of managers. We were the owners.

Some questions were raised. How can we take such a drastic action, and what will the market think about it? Who will run the company once the CEO is gone? QRG firmly said that we would get the answers only after Griswold was gone. We had to remove the managerial obstacles, or it would be too late. His confidence in our ability to manage Sylvania was inspiring.

On a cold, foggy morning, as QRG and I drove together, as we did every working day when we were in Delhi, from our house in Old Delhi's Civil Lines to the Noida office, we finally agreed on how to let Griswold go.

We decided that we needed to meet all the senior managers in Sylvania in Noida right after the Christmas holidays. The date we fixed for this was 5 January 2009. I asked Griswold to come a couple of days early, on 3 January, as there were important matters to discuss.

On the appointed day, he came to my office where I told him it would be best if we were to go our separate ways. There was no reaction from him, no thumping of the table. He was clearly dejected and offered to help us negotiate with the banks, which I politely declined. He had coffee with QRG and by noon he was out of our office, on his way back to the hotel. Such meetings are always short. When you decide to part ways, there is little to say. That same night Griswold left for New York.

We had to pay two years' compensation to Griswold, as it was written in his contract signed with the earlier owners. His exit cost us a lot of money, but in retrospect, it was a decision that had to be taken. We had to bite the bullet.

We were now ready to talk directly with Sylvania's managers.

SEVENTEEN

Tough Talk

In August 2008, we moved into our new office on Noida Expressway which connects Noida with Greater Noida. QRG Towers, which was spread on a three-and-a-half-acre plot, had cost us in excess of Rs 60 crore to build. It conveyed to the world that we had arrived, and we were not some shady corporation operating out of an unknown alley of Old Delhi.

It was in QRG Towers that the eventful meetings of 5 and 6 January were held. Naturally, it was a big occasion for all of us. We were excited, but we were also nervous. QRG had decided to address the senior managers of Sylvania directly. We had no idea what he would tell them.

QRG strode into the meeting with confidence, even aplomb. He seemed sure of himself. He gave the impression that he had the solution for each of the problems that plagued Sylvania and our group. He swaggered into the room and announced that he would be transparent.

He admitted that it was his folly to stay away from Sylvania for nineteen months. As a promoter, he should have been in the thick of things. But he would rectify the mistake. He told the managers who had come from different countries that Havells would change things at Sylvania—and fast. 'You people,' he told them, 'are used to driving on shiny roads, while we drive on roads with potholes. As Sylvania has also got into a bumpy drive, let me handle the situation.'

QRG talked tough and did not mince words. Those who had come thinking there would be some long lecture and little else were in for a rude shock. He asked each of them how they could downsize. If somebody gave a figure that QRG felt was too low, he would immediately be challenged. When the occasion demanded, QRG could be tough as nails.

What helped was that Havells, in the slowdown of 2008, had also downsized its rolls by 15 per cent. This had given him some idea of the flab that old offices accumulate, which can be removed with surgical precision without affecting performance.

Slowly, it dawned on the Sylvania managers that QRG meant business. I saw the changed expressions of the managers—from doubt to excitement—and my fears vanished. The suggestions on downsizing, and also on how to improve profitability, began to come in torrents.

The meeting was a resounding success.

Sylvania's executives themselves pieced together a revival plan. Each head of a division, factory or location, provided us with the number of excess employees. They gave us concrete numbers of the possible reductions in manpower. The figures were reasonable and achievable as they came from those who were directly in charge of the divisions. In a matter of two days, we had a workable blueprint in front of us—one that could be implemented immediately.

After the meeting, we were confident we could tackle Sylvania and turn it around. We then approached the bankers with our blueprint. We told them that we had not mismanaged the company. In fact, we had delegated too much; so, we shouldn't be judged by Sylvania's bad performance. We convinced the lenders that we could prove our mettle in six months.

We promised we could complete a part of the restructuring within this time period and show results. The bankers still wanted us to put in money upfront as additional equity to show our seriousness. We said we would not do that, but we could free up cash internally through deep cuts in other costs.

Since we were sincere and honest, and we had a plan that seemed workable, the lenders agreed to watch the performance for another six months.

This gave birth to two projects—Operation Phoenix (the first phase of the restructuring which would tackle costs that were lower and could be cut quickly) and Operation Parakaram (this was the second phase and was about deep cuts, in countries like Belgium and Germany where we had to negotiate with the labour unions) which aimed to turn around Sylvania within eighteen months.

However, the first task was to show results in the first six months that would please the lenders and force them to work with us.

Essentially, the global bankers of the lighting company were worried about the payments of their loans, as Sylvania's profits slipped into the red and revenues took a tumble. We told the lenders that we had invested €80 million to buy the company, and we would not allow the huge investment to go to waste. So, they should not worry about a smaller amount, i.e. repayment of the next instalment of the loans. But the bankers were emotionless; they asked us to pump in an additional €36 million. It was an amount we did not wish to risk.

Somehow, we convinced them about our seriousness and our plans to turn the company around. Within a few months, we showed results and the bankers agreed on a workable plan with us. We estimated that the restructuring plan would cost €36 million. The bankers agreed to defer repayments for twenty-four months which gave us a cushion of €24 million; we pumped in another €12 million from Havells. This was enough to immediately boost the overall cash flows.

Later, we got all the loans refinanced by another consortium of banks that comprised HSBC, ICICI Bank and Standard Chartered.

However, there were the regular cash management problems at Sylvania. Our loan agreement said that we could not raise more loans, and our additional fund requirement should flow in through equity. Since we had risked enough, we did not wish to increase our exposure. Another alternative had to be found and we spotted a loophole of sorts.

'We thought that if we got extra credit period from our creditors, i.e. got additional time to pay our vendors, it would translate into additional funds with us, but it wouldn't be categorized as loans. But the question was, how could we do this in Sylvania? We formed a company in Hong Kong to centralize our purchases of raw materials and components from China. In a sense, Sylvania gave its purchase orders to the Hong Kong entity, which procured the products from China, and sold them to Sylvania.

'The Chinese suppliers gave forty-five days credit to the Hong Kong firm. But two banks, HSBC and Standard Chartered, gave the Hong Kong firm 180 days' credit to pay the loans it extended to pay the Chinese firms. In short, the Hong Kong firm got a loan for an additional 135 days (180 minus 45). This translated into extra cash of €30 million! The two banks were happy with the arrangement because they earned interest on the money extended to the Hong Kong firm, which was a safe client,' Rajesh Gupta would remember later.

We looked at ways to cut costs further, and the measures to do so had been suggested by Sylvania's managers at the 5 January meeting. We reduced manpower by over 40 per cent, from 3800 to just over 2200. Most of the people offloaded were in non-productive jobs—accounts, information technology—and redundant factory staff. Some of these and other back-office operations were shifted to India, where a Sylvania cell was formed.

Quite a few of the senior managers too were shown the door. Of the sixty who had come to Delhi after we completed the acquisition, all but five were given pink slips!

Fortunately for us, the lay-offs did not result in any protest or strike by the employees and unions in the various countries. Everything went smoothly; we followed the labour laws in each of the countries where people were retrenched. We made contractual payments according to the laws and before the due dates.

Unviable factories in Brazil and Costa Rica were shut down. The work at the UK plant was suspended and the production work was shifted to the Havells plants in India. The benefit of the latter move was that the Indian labour costs comprised 4–5 per cent of overall costs, compared to over 20 per cent in the UK.

Other logistical changes were implemented. For example, Sylvania had twelve warehouses to stock inventories of the final products in Europe; these were collapsed into two—in the United Kingdom and France. A few employees felt that this move would increase freight costs and delay deliveries, which did happen in the first few weeks.

But we found solutions to get around these issues. We told distributors that instead of deliveries every day, we would do them once in three days. Thus, we could combine deliveries to a certain region that included several countries. Our logistics costs came down from 12 per cent of the total to 6 per cent.

There were other fires too that we had to put out.

Strategically, we figured that there was a mismatch between the positioning and pricing of Sylvania's products. While the brand had credibility in terms of quality and performance, prices were too low and the company operated at wafer-thin margins, even incurring losses in certain product categories. We decided to change this mindset. We asked the managers to look at the prices of all the products.

We sought to make Sylvania's managers understand that we were not in the commodity business and, hence, we were not necessarily in the volumes game. We had to behave like a branded company from now on, and charge a premium on each product.

Tactically, it meant that everyone had to focus on margins; every product category had to be a profit centre. To achieve this, if prices had to be raised, so be it. The managers were asked to revisit, tinker and change prices of products in all the countries where Sylvania's products were sold.

We changed the decision-making process in Sylvania. We did away with the regional heads who looked at several countries together or larger geographical areas. National-level managers, or country heads, were given more powers and flexibility to take decisions that suited the local environment.

Accountability was fixed at the country level. Margins were fixed for each country, and the respective heads were given freedom as well as support from Havells to take these decisions. All issues were discussed and debated openly with the country managers. Nothing was pushed down their throats.

Within months, Sylvania's managers began to think like us. They were now in sync with Havells's corporate philosophy, which empowers the managers, yet keeps them accountable. More importantly, as QRG would stress, a single, and identical, message should go out to each and every employee. All employees had to think similarly, in the manner that we did. There should be no confusion and no obfuscation in the decision-making process at all levels.

I travelled every month to reinforce this singular message. We called 300 sales employees for a meeting in Frankfurt to reiterate the core philosophy. We had to earn margins; we could not pursue top-line growth at any cost; the bottom line was critical. In addition, the employees were free to take decisions but they had to adhere to their quantitative and qualitative targets.

The meeting was addressed by QRG, Ameet, some other senior members of the team and me. Some of the teams came fully charged up. The one from the UK came with a cricket bat. The one from the US brought a baseball bat with signatures and commitments on it. The only challenge in the meeting was the language as more than 60 per cent of the attendees did not speak or understand English. Just like a UN summit, translators were arranged and attendees could then listen to live translation in their own language.

This is the kind of person QRG was. He was keen to personally know all the key managers and employees in the company. In fact, during the Sylvania crisis, he would ask my views on different individuals, their strengths and weaknesses, and their performances.

Whenever he met them, he could see through them, and get instinctive vibes—positive or negative—about them. If he didn't feel good about someone, he would clinically let him/her leave. If the feeling was good, QRG would soon chalk out a long-term future for him/her within the organization.

In one of the meetings, he saw a manager glancing at his laptop several times. He snapped, 'If we don't discuss issues seriously, and we don't listen to each other, all your work on the laptop will be a complete waste.' For QRG, laptops and mobile phones were nothing more than distractions.

Our efforts yielded fruits.

As *Business Today* reported, 'The results soon began to show in 2010–11. Sylvania made a net profit of €7 million on revenues of €449.4 million. Since then, profits have grown steadily—€10.2 million in 2011–12 and €30.5 million in 2012–13, although revenues stayed somewhat flat (€449.4 million in 2011–12 and €439.9 million in 2012–13). The company has seven factories (it closed one more in the UK in 2009) and a workforce of 2200 people in fifty countries.'

What's important is that we spent €4 million less on the restructuring than the original estimate of €36 million.

In the years that followed, we scaled down the factories in Europe and South America. We fed these markets out of China. We started a fifty-fifty partnership in China, called Havells Jiangsu, which makes lamps, LEDs and fixtures for Europe. The Sylvania acquisition came with a laboratory in China. It was small, conducted some basic tests and was staffed with expats. We expanded its scope, made it bigger and installed an all-Chinese team.

I have often been asked why we haven't launched Sylvania in China and India. The reason is very simple—it is not easy to build a business from scratch. In China, we would have to acquire a brand that would give us a lateral entry into the market. In India, we already have Havells, so launching Sylvania didn't make any sense.

This, in spite of the fact that we had to exert ourselves to use the Sylvania brand in India. As I mentioned earlier, there was a company called Laxman & Sylvania already operating in India. After a good run that lasted up to the eighties, the company had gone into decline in the nineties. Its founder, Laxman Agarwal, had died and his family was running it. We had come to know that they had licensed the brand to somebody else.

Since we owned the brand, we told the family that they couldn't do so. Agarwal's widow was adamant, though we tried to convince her that their case was flimsy and would be thrown out by the courts in no time. After a while, through a common friend who lived in Civil Lines, we did an out-of-court settlement with her, which involved a payout of about Rs 1 crore.

In spite of not entering the sunrise markets of China and India, the Sylvania business stabilized quickly. Sylvania, and its amazing turnaround, was a huge feather in QRG's hat.

We put in place a new management structure for Sylvania, which was different from Havells's because we are not involved in day-to-day management. First, we closed down the office in New York and moved the head office to Germany. It was located outside Frankfurt in a sleepy town called Raunheim. I must admit that it was very convenient for us whenever we travelled to Frankfurt since it was not too far from the airport. However, it became difficult for us to get good people there.

In contrast, our London office was always abuzz with activity. So, in 2011, we moved the head office for Europe to London. The office we established in London is lively and overlooks a magnificent cricket field. That is where Sylvania's European head was based. We don't have a similar point person for South America because Sylvania doesn't have a centralized structure there.

Despite initial apprehensions, we were not only able to retain most of the erstwhile Frankfurt team but consolidated the senior management with further diversity and deeper industry knowledge. London is a confluence of cultures and nationalities, with an open and inclusive work environment acting as a magnet for professionals across Europe.

Christian Schraft, the European head, reported to Rajiv Goel, the PwC partner who joined us in 2009, in Noida. But we also have direct access to each country head. None of the country heads are Indian. In fact, we have sent only one person from India to our London office.

There is an interesting story about how Schraft joined us. As I mentioned earlier, Osram, owned by Siemens, had the rights for the Sylvania brand in North America. It came to our notice that it had licensed the brand to manufacturers in China for products like television sets and home appliances.

But China was our territory. We demanded royalty and also said the licensing would have to happen through us. They obviously did not agree and the matter went to arbitration in Paris in 2011.

However, in 2012, Osram did an out-of-court settlement with us—we gave up all claims on royalty, though all licensing was done by us, in return for which Osram paid us $38 million. Schraft was the head of strategy for Osram and led the negotiations with us. When we were looking for a European head, Schraft was one of the many people who applied. We felt a certain degree of comfort with Schraft, so we hired him. That's how he came on board.

A key element of the Sylvania turnaround was the downsizing. It is important to mention that it was against QRG's nature to downsize. He always believed in adding quality people to the organization, to the extent of paranoia.

There were times that he liked a job applicant but couldn't find a slot for him. He would nevertheless hire him, even if it added to the bench strength, to ensure that there be no talent crunch in the company.

In 2011, QRG tasked the senior people of Havells to go to the top B-schools in the country and hire 200 MBAs— these people, he argued, would carry Havells forward. He wanted to build another line of defence.

But business exigencies also demanded downsizing. QRG would take all decisions, good or bad, to serve the company's interests. He always said that he wanted to save the company first rather than a few people. If he agreed to trim the rolls, it was with a certain degree of reluctance.

Crises generally comes in pairs. Or if you are a believer in Murphy's Law, then you know that if things have to go wrong, everything will go wrong at the same time. This is exactly what happened to us in 2008. As the Sylvania crisis began to unfold and become a disaster, Havells too went through a difficult time.

EIGHTEEN

Securing the Homeland

Initially, we, as well as other Indian businessmen, thought that India had weathered the storm of the global financial crisis. We had managed to safely swim ashore. In the first eight months of 2008, our domestic business seemed to be in better shape than before, despite alarms of a second Great Depression and cataclysmic shifts in the US and European economies.

We had all gone on a holiday to Shimla, the summer capital of India in colonial times, in October 2008. During this holiday, QRG and I discussed a few expansion plans in the near future. We were optimistic and gung-ho. It was then that we realized that the tide had begun to turn.

The global financial cyclone struck India as well. Every business was in turmoil. The prices of our products began to dip 5–10 per cent every month, thanks to the slowdown. Although this was balanced a bit by the fall in the prices of raw materials, like copper and aluminium, it proved to be a double whammy for us.

We had huge stocks of the two input metals, which we had purchased at the earlier higher prices. In October 2008, copper prices slumped by 30 per cent within a month. The fall continued. So, we had to reduce the prices of our final products, and still use raw materials we had bought at the high prices.

I had never seen anything like this before. I had not joined the business in 1991, when the previous economic crisis unfolded, and the 1996–97 Asian Currency Crisis did not impact India for too long. But the domestic situation towards the end of 2008 triggered full-blown panic.

In one of our morning meetings, QRG asked a few rapid-fire questions. What were our monthly sales and profit margins today? I said Rs 180 crore a month with a margin of 10 per cent. What would happen if sales went down to Rs 150 crore? We could still break even. What if they were down to Rs 100 crore? I answered that we would incur losses at those levels.

QRG insisted that he wanted Havells to make profits even if monthly sales went down to Rs 100 crore. He said that he wanted to transform Havells into a company that could keep its head above water even if revenues slid 40–50 per cent in no time. Havells, he maintained, should be able to survive even if the country's economic growth was lower than 5 per cent.

The lessons we learnt in those days and the company we rejigged in 2008–09 helped us in 2012–14, when economic growth actually plummeted to 5 per cent for two years in a row.

On one of our usual morning car rides to the office, I asked QRG if he was serious about the Rs 100 crore discussions we had. He said 'yes'. 'In that case,' I told him,

'Havells would have to cut costs.' 'So, let's do it; let's work out a new blueprint to achieve this objective,' he said with a sigh.

As soon as we reached the office, I spread this message to my colleagues, and the senior team went into crisis management mode. All our brains worked in a bid to tackle the new issues.

Within days we called the heads of the various factories and brands. We told them upfront that we had grown too fast, too soon in the past few years. But the boom days were now over. Slower growth had made us realize that our expenses had ballooned faster than our revenues in the past few years.

In our bid to chase growth and a better future, we had chaotically and randomly added to the sales workforce and to the number of branch offices. This was not tenable.

We were left with no choice but to trim our rolls. It was an unpleasant task but it had to be done for the company's sake. While most companies are nonchalant about laying off people, it just wasn't in our DNA.

During those days, we looked carefully at the people we had employed in the recent past. I came across a group of twenty-five to thirty recruits, who had arrived at the Noida office for training workshops. I spoke to them and found them not up to the mark. Clearly, our recent hiring was inconsistent and had been done merely to meet targets without taking into account their abilities and talents.

The same was true in the case of the factories, where expansion at any cost had led to huge expenses. For example, the finished goods' inventories were Rs 320 crore, too high against the monthly sales of Rs 180 crore. This figure had to be brought down.

For the next two months, the organization was on tenterhooks. Overall expenses were slashed by 40 per cent; the sales force was cut by a similar percentage while the number of employees in the various factories was brought down by 30 per cent. By December 2008, inventory levels were down to Rs 130 crore. The big positive outcome was that Havells felt lighter in terms of both manpower and finances.

As QRG had predicted, monthly sales came tumbling down—Rs 150 crore in October 2008, Rs 137 crore each in November and December. The action we had taken had been timely.

By February 2009, things had quietened down. This was for two reasons—one, the Indian economy picked up despite the global recession; and two, Havells underwent a violent surgery. But I still shudder to think of those three or four months. The employees were scared, to say the least; they thought we were corporate demons.

I still remember a day when QRG and I took the elevator to our respective offices on the fifth floor of QRG Towers and heard a few employees talk about the problems in the metering business. We realized that these people were still on our rolls, though we had exited the meters business. Did we really want them? It was decided that they had no work and hence were a burden Havells could not afford.

I must admit that it created some sort of a scare in the company. The non-performers, *lalli challi*, in QRG's vocabulary, became vulnerable. The high-performers had no reason to worry but even they did not want to bump into us in the corridors. If they saw us walking towards them, they would quickly change direction; if they saw us taking the same elevator, they would disappear and wait for the next one.

Obviously, the atmosphere changed when the Indian economy bounced back to 8.6 per cent growth in 2009–10, from 6.5 per cent in the previous year. The growth rate was 9.7 per cent in 2007–08, the highest since 1988–89 (9.9 per cent). Everyone in the office, including us, heaved a sigh of relief.

When the economic turmoil engulfed the country in 2011–12, and the economy slowed down to 6.4 per cent, we were better prepared for the crisis. Even a further nosedive to 5 per cent in 2012–13 and 2013–14, respectively, did not force us to panic. We had been there, done that. We knew internally that even if sales slumped 50 per cent, we would still remain profitable.

However, this was not the case across India Inc. Most companies and almost all the employees in the organized sector seemed to be gripped by fear in 2012–14. Most companies went overboard cutting expenses without a thought for the negative impact their actions were having. People were pink-slipped randomly to meet cost targets. Investments, increments and additional expenditures were stalled or postponed.

I feel this happened for two reasons. The first was that the business community, as well as most of the working middle class, had not witnessed a sustained slowdown since 1990. In fact, before 2012, there were no two consecutive years when economic growth was lower than the previous year. In a nutshell, if the economy faltered in any year, it grew at a faster clip or the same rate the next year.

Even the worst year in this period—1991–92 when the growth rate was a mere 1.4 per cent—was followed by a good one when in 1992–93, the figure was a decent 5.4 per cent.

Therefore, no one believed in a slowdown that could last for so many years. Everyone thought that India had some sort of inherent ability to remain immune to either global or domestic crises. The Asian Currency Crisis of 1997, which created havoc among Asian Tigers, impacted us for a year, as did the Global Financial Crisis of 2008, which almost ruined the economies of developed nations.

Between 1990 and 2012, India weathered several local economic storms—in 1991, 2000 and 2002. In these instances, the economy revved up after a year.

The second reason for this blind faith in the Indian economy was the fact that between 2003 and 2012, it has grown by over 6 per cent each year. In seven out of these nine years, the growth rate was 7 per cent and above. Of the six years between 2005 and 2011, the economy took off at over 8.5 per cent a year in five of them; in three consecutive years (2005–06, 2006–07 and 2007–08), the respective figures were over 9.5 per cent.

Most people felt that God had ordained that India would grow at least 8 per cent a year. In the minds of the policy makers, even if they did not do anything, 8 per cent was a given; they had to only think of how to translate it into double-digit growth rates. This is why, Pranab Mukherjee, the then finance minister, predicted in 2010 that India will achieve this China-like growth within five years. Even the planning commission toyed with the idea of targeting an average annual growth rate of 10 per cent during the Twelfth Plan Period (2012–2017); this was subsequently reduced to 9 per cent in the final report.

The economic slowdown, and the way we negotiated it, brought out QRG's ability to adapt to change. Havells came out of the crises leaner and fitter. If something like that were to happen again, our blueprint for survival was ready.

NINETEEN

Brand Sutra

Any management student, and every professional manager, knows that there is a distinction between the life cycle of a product and that of a brand. A product life cycle usually follows the typical span of introduction, growth, maturity and decline, much like the birth to death cycle of any living organism.

However, a brand's life is more complex, and its journey over time can take several twists and turns. Design thinking and innovation guru Idris Mootee's analysis succinctly captures this process. In an article in September 2007, he detailed how brands evolve during their lifetimes.

Most start as mere products, and grow to become service brands. 'Over years of brand building effort and market presence they become either a category brand, which is defined as having leading market share within a category, a personality brand, which establishes a strong brand personality that consumers identify with, or an experience brand, which goes beyond traditional service and product excellence with a strong sense of uniqueness . . .

'After being extremely successful, these brands become cash generating trademarks. They will then sometime be moved up one level and become a corporate brand (the brand name becomes the corporation), or a global brand, expanding geographically to become a global dominant leader,' explained Mootee.

Havells's journey followed a similar pattern. It actually started as a B2B brand. The buyers of our industrial switchgears were government departments, building contractors and offices. Our marketing was thus tailored to that market.

To sell to our buyers, we used to hold conferences and meetings. This was, in essence, technical communication. Questions would be asked about the products, which we would answer to the best of our ability. Of course, we got all the quality certifications that were required in order to get empanelled with various government departments and agencies.

We were required to stay in touch with our buyers constantly. These would include personnel from the public works department, military engineering services, etc. Since their numbers weren't large, QRG had built a personal rapport with them. Up to the mid-nineties, as I have said earlier, these relationships were, by and large, all about personal rapport. It was only later that big money started to change hands—something we were distinctly uncomfortable with.

Apart from seminars, we put up some hoardings here and there, and also did some point-of-sale promotion. This was to create some kind of a connection if a buyer came to the shop undecided. The fact that QRG had close relations with most dealers ensured that they pushed Havells to such buyers.

For the dealers, and also our buyers, we used to print brochures and pamphlets about our products. Even in the early days, QRG saw to it that these were of a high quality. He had hired a dedicated professional to work on brochures and point-of-sale displays. In the nineties, we also put out some advertisements in newspapers, but there was nothing of significance.

To be fair, in the seventies, Indian companies were focused on production and their brand consciousness was low. It was the age of shortage—whatever was produced was sold right away. Cars and scooters used to command waiting periods of six months to a year. Naturally, nobody needed to worry about brand power.

In 1977, things took a turn for the worse when Coca-Cola and IBM were asked to leave the country by the then industry minister, George Fernandes, the firebrand trade union leader and socialist. These were mighty brands, and one fine day they just vanished from the shelves in India!

But winds of change were soon blowing across the country's political landscape. When Rajiv Gandhi pushed through the first wave of economic reforms as the prime minister in 1984, with relaxations on imports and clearances for collaborations between Indian firms and multinational corporations, the focus of Indian companies for the first time turned on brands and the boost they could give to business.

In several sectors, especially the automobile sector, companies vied to find foreign partners to launch hybrid brands—Maruti Suzuki, Kinetic Honda, Hero Honda,

Bajaj Kawasaki, TVS Suzuki, DCM Toyota, Swaraj Mazda et al. In other categories, like personal computers and electronics, the focus was to import components and assemble the final Indian-branded products in the country.

QRG watched the emergence of these brands with fascination. He found particularly mesmerizing the high-decibel advertising of Hero Honda (now called Hero MotoCorp). Its 'Fill it, shut it, forget it' campaign, which emphasized its high-fuel economy, was an instant hit. Within no time, it had emerged the undisputed leader of the motorcycle market.

This partly explains the overseas collaborations we stitched together in the eighties. The products were co-branded, Havells Geyer and Havells Dorman Smith, for instance, which gave us a certain halo in the marketplace. We took the first step towards becoming a B2C company when we started making MCBs for households in collaboration with Geyer of Germany in the eighties. Apart from government departments and builders, small households had also become our customers.

At that time, houses were built on a stand-alone basis—the concept of large gated communities had not taken shape. However, households were often influenced by the electrician—most of them would buy the switches he recommended. In case of a bigger project, the decision would be taken by the engineer or architect in charge. They were the people who influenced the choices of the homeowner.

In this scenario, all we could do was work with the dealer to push our brand. Technologically, all the products in the market were similar. In many cases, the buyer would come to the retail store with his mind made up, influenced by the advice of the engineer or the electrician. In quite a few cases, the dealer was able to push the brand. 'Try this brand; it is of a very good quality,' he would tell the buyer.

The next big step in our evolution as a B2C company was Crabtree modular switches. Here, again, the buyers were households. In spite of our limited budgets, we were able to create a fair amount of awareness for the brand. QRG knew the brand had the potential to grow big, and that's why we bought it for the Indian subcontinent when the opportunity presented itself.

In those days, our advertising budgets were really small. Even as late as in 2003, for instance, we spent all of Rs 2.5 crore on promotion. This, mind you, included the money we spent on seminars and events—the actual media expenses were still lower.

That was the year we got into fans and lighting—a purely B2C category. Our advertising costs began to inch up.

That was also the time when QRG started to nudge us towards a stronger brand play. He would often ask why we couldn't sell switchgear, cables and wire—all under the same brand. Why did we have to sell them like commodities? Wasn't it true that if we branded them, we would get a better price?

Everybody saw the logic of his argument but felt that it was too bold for its time. After all, that was the industry norm. Few were prepared to go against conventional wisdom. But QRG wouldn't give up. Finally, we called Hindustan Thompson Associates (HTA), the leading advertising agency of the time, to devise a communication strategy.

The agency had started out as J. Walter Thompson in India in 1929. In 1970, it changed its name to HTA after the Indian government ruled that no fully owned foreign agency would be allowed to handle public sector accounts. The agency not only changed its name but also got in some Indian shareholders. According to one account, almost 20 per cent of its business came from the public sector that it didn't want to let go off.

Subsequently, it reverted to its old name, JWT India. Martin Sorrell's WPP owned 74 per cent of it and it was led by Mike Khanna, its well-respected CEO. (Khanna passed away in June 2015 at the age of seventy-six.)

HTA sent a team of executives to meet us. At the outset, I told them that our budgets were very small and they may not find it worthwhile to do business with us. They asked me what kind of money I had in mind. I said we could stretch our annual budget to Rs 7 or 8 crore, which was still puny when compared to FMCG, consumer electronics and automobile companies. They said HTA had a special agency called Thompson Connect to deal with such small accounts and therefore this agency would work with us.

Thompson Connect made two films for us, one on wires and the other on MCBs, which were shown on television. We got some traction, though not much.

Then something happened which totally derailed all our plans. In the quarter that ended in March 2004, our profits slipped, though the turnover had risen. After three good quarters in the financial year, we had taken a hard knock in the fourth quarter.

Though our share price was languishing and was indifferent to the results we declared every quarter, questions began to be raised internally about our plans. One of these was—should we increase our advertising budgets when profits were in a bind? It was seen as a luxury we just could not afford.

The naysayers had their way. We rolled back the campaigns. The TV ads were withdrawn.

Somehow, QRG was not convinced. One quarter of bad results couldn't derail our long-term plans, he argued. He would often give me the example of Hero Honda, how it had booked huge space in the print as well as electronic media. 'Why can't we do the same?' he would often ask.

My stock answer was that Hero Honda made a pure consumer product, while we did not. He would withdraw but I could sense that he was restless about it. Somehow, I knew that unless we also had large advertising budgets, he would not be at ease. The only question was when?

In 2004, we hired Vijay Narayanan from LG.

Sometime in the mid-nineties, LG (it was known as Lucky Goldstar then), the South Korean chaebol (a large family-owned business), had sent a high-powered team to India to assess business prospects. The odds were stacked against the company—low awareness of its brand, poor perception of Korean technology, etc. But the team felt the Japanese were not too interested in India because Europe and the US were their primary focus. As a result, homegrown Indian brands had become complacent.

According to one account, it also found out that education was very high on the agenda of Indians. The team members knew that it was education that had transformed South Korea from a poor, agrarian country into a developed industrial powerhouse in a matter of decades. The same would happen in India, the team reported to its bosses back home. The LG top brass were convinced and made up their mind to enter India. As rules did not allow a fully owned subsidiary, it first tried its luck with Bestavision and then with Chandra Kant Birla. Finally, in 1997, when the foreign ownership rules were relaxed, it came on its own.

Around the same time, another Korean company had India on its radar. It came to my attention in the middle of 1994, that the Dhoots of Videocon (the family had its roots in sugar and cotton, and later diversified into consumer electronics, and oil and gas) were approached by Samsung to sell its consumer electronics in India. The company had proposed a joint venture that could source products from Videocon's factories at Aurangabad in Maharashtra, according to the same account.

Quantitative research threw up no surprises. Unaided brand awareness about Samsung was close to zero, aided awareness was a tad better at 7 per cent. People thought the Japanese were the masters of all technology, and the Koreans were at best imitators. Digging deeper, the Dhoots found deep dissatisfaction among consumers with multinational (Sony, Sanyo, National, Philips) as well as Indian brands (Videocon, Onida, BPL et al).

The consumers' aspiration and awareness levels were high, but the quality of the technology made available to them was low. And there was no indication that any brand would invest in the latest technology. After-sales services did not exist.

The Dhoots knew there was a big gap that could be exploited. With better technology, contemporary products and a customer-friendly disposition, the market could be entered into. If Samsung did well, they argued, their factories at Aurangabad would run at full capacity, and whenever the foreign investment rules were further liberalized, they could sell their stake to the Korean chaebol and make a neat pile of money. Quickly, they formed a 49:51 company with Samsung. The year was 1995.

Together, LG and Samsung heralded the Korean invasion of India. Within no time, they had snatched business away from all other makers of consumer electronics—Indian as well as Japanese and western players—across categories like televisions, refrigerators, washing machines and microwave ovens. Their marketing muscle was like nothing India had seen before.

In the Korean tsunami that ensued, many established brands got swept away. The two companies rewrote the rules of marketing in India. Advertising budgets reached unheard-of levels. Marketing gimmickry hit its peak.

It was to draw some of that talent that we brought LG's Narayanan on board.

One day, at 9 a.m., several weeks after the Sylvania takeover, QRG called Narayanan to his office with budget sheets on annual expenditures related to marketing and communications. QRG asked Narayanan a simple question, 'How much money do you wish to spend in 2007?'

Narayanan was a little perplexed, not knowing what was coming next. Although advertising budgets had increased in the last few years, the amounts were puny compared to FMCG firms and even some of our competitors. Our annual advertising budget was Rs 17 crore in 2005 and Rs 18 crore the next year, a meagre rise of 6 per cent—that too on a small base. Keeping that in mind, Narayanan's answer was Rs 18–20 crore.

QRG now asked him a second question, 'How much money do you need to spend to make the Havells brand much bigger than it is?' The query stumped Narayanan. He had never given it a thought earlier, as he had assumed that budgets on advertising and promotion would continue to grow at the usual pace, and may be slightly more in percentage terms than the previous years.

So, he simply plucked a figure from thin air. 'Rs 80 crore,' Narayanan said, not knowing how QRG would react.

To his surprise, QRG did not bat an eyelid. He did not pause to think and brood over it. He gave him the go-ahead with a small caveat—Narayanan had to be sure that he spent the entire amount. Wasting no further time, QRG asked Narayanan to prepare a new annual advertising plan. That was it. No more discussions. Narayanan returned shell-shocked to his cabin.

This was quintessential QRG. Once he took a decision, he expected it to be implemented immediately. He did not question the intelligence of the manager concerned, who drew up the plan, and delegated full responsibility to the person concerned. He then monitored only its progress, and made mid-course corrections, and only if they were required on an urgent basis.

I remember Narayanan went into a tizzy that morning. I was not in town, which complicated matters for him. On the one hand, he knew QRG's words were sacrosanct, and the new advertising budget was final. On the other hand, he was in a state of disbelief and wanted to talk to me to get a confirmation.

More importantly, Narayanan had come from LG where advertising budgets would be discussed ad nauseam for days, weeks, even months, before they were approved. The passing of the budgets was a bureaucratic process that required Excel spreadsheets, PowerPoint presentations, and discussions between managers from different divisions and hierarchies. At Havells, it had happened within seconds. He was not used to it.

A budget of Rs 80 crore, out of which Rs 50 crore was set aside for media buying, was indeed a big deal for us. In 2006–07, we had made profit before tax of Rs 120 crore, and we expected to end 2007–08 with Rs 180 crore. I was in total agreement with QRG, though some people within the company felt it was not wise to bump up the budget like this—it would take a toll on our bottom line.

But, as always, QRG had made up his mind and nothing would make him change it. He had created great excitement among Narayanan's team—nobody could puncture their enthusiasm. In fact, it became infectious.

It was the end of summer, and the fan season was more or less over. Still, we decided to go ahead with our plans. This was also the time we shifted from JWT to Lowe Lintas.

What made us decide to switch was that Lowe Lintas's then national creative director, R. Balakrishnan, (he is now the chairman and chief creative officer), came for the meetings and assured us that he would personally work on the Havells account. This was important for us—in all the years that we worked with JWT, Mike Khanna hadn't met us even once.

Balki, at the time, was the rising star of the advertising world. He had created several successful campaigns and had just released his first film, *Cheeni Kum*, which had Amitabh Bachchan and Tabu in lead roles. The film had won critical acclaim. 'One thing advertising teaches you is not to be self-indulgent,' he had said in an interaction with a newspaper after the film's release. 'Maybe I too will become esoteric. But my genetic structure is that I am hard-core crass, commercial.' That suited us fine!

We made it very clear in the discussions that we wanted our advertisements to stand out—which was necessary because the product categories per se, switches and wires, were boring. That, we all agreed, would only happen if the advertisement films had a strong storyline and were shot with perfection. They could be serious, they could be funny, but they had to be absolutely amazing.

Balki created two outstanding campaigns for us—one of which was directed by Balki's film-maker wife, Gauri Shinde (she is best known for her 2012 film, *English Vinglish*). The first was the '*shock laga*' (got an electric shock) series, which highlighted the safety and quality of Havells switches.

With the use of ordinary life's humour, and average middle-class characters, the 'shock laga' TV advertisements appealed to most viewers. They laughed at them, they associated with the events (many of them had indeed got a shock using electrical products) in the ads, and we managed to convey the realization that safety was an important factor.

The second series the agency created was the 'wires that don't catch fire' one. This was more emotional in nature, although it still focused on quality and safety. This was an outstanding ad and my personal favourite.

This ad is about a child who sees his mother's fingers being burnt while she makes chapattis. In the film made by Shinde, the boy walks out, makes a forked implement out of Havells wire, and gives it to her for her to hold the hot food with. The mother happily and proudly uses the new implement to make the chapattis. The tag line was simply 'Havells—the wires that don't catch fire'. Many viewers, including our consumers, remembered these ads many years after they were shown on TV.

Our entire media strategy was driven by our focus on TV. QRG was completely on board for this approach. It was clear that people had turned fully to the electronic media to get their daily dose of news and entertainment. Print media, on the other hand, was on the decline. The reach of the electronic media at the time was many times more than that of print.

Narayanan suggested cricket. Ask any communication specialist and he will tell you that only three things sell in India—Bollywood, cricket and religion. Our obvious choice was the gentleman's game. India, even then, was the nerve centre of global cricket.

Fortunately for us, and unfortunately for the millions of Indian cricket fans, cricket was in a temporary decline in 2007. At the World Cup in the West Indies, India had done poorly. All of a sudden, there was talk of fatigue with cricket. The fans had turned against their icons. This resulted in advertising slots becoming cheaper.

Mindshare, our media buying agency, told us that the upcoming series in England was going cheap. What would have cost up to Rs 10 crore in better times was available for as little as Rs 6 crore. I mentioned it to QRG. For a moment, he felt it was expensive. But my enthusiasm rubbed off on him and he agreed.

This proved to be a great break for us. After the tour of England, India went on to win the inaugural T20 World Cup organized by the International Cricket Council in South Africa. Contrary to expectations, a star-depleted Indian team, led by its young captain, Mahendra Singh Dhoni, did well in match after match and ultimately lifted the trophy. What had been written off as a low viewer engagement event went on to break all records of viewership! We were on a roll.

Soon, another opportunity came our way. In 2008, the Board of Control for Cricket in India (BCCI) launched the Indian Premier League, modelled loosely on the English Premier League. Led by the mercurial Lalit Modi, it was the kind of grand-scale cricket event that had never been seen before—not even in the Kerry Packer days. IPL had glamour, sport, big money—a heady mix of everything.

Once the BCCI announced the launch of the first IPL season in 2008, we debated whether to advertise for this new T20 league. Most people favoured the association since they felt that viewership for T20 matches would zoom after India won the first T20 World Cup.

We had prepared the TV ads to be aired during the IPL matches but at the last minute we pulled out. We, like many other advertisers, were not totally convinced about the success of a T20 format among city franchises, owned by a mix of celebrities and businessmen, where neither the fans nor the players would have any team loyalty, at least in the first season.

Then we saw the first IPL match between Royal Challengers Bangalore, owned by liquor baron Vijay Mallya, and Kolkata Knight Riders, part owned by Bollywood stars Shah Rukh Khan and Juhi Chawla. Although it was a one-sided game—RCB was bowled out for 82, and lost by a huge margin of 140 runs—it electrified the audience. Brendon McCullum scored a swashbuckling 158 not out for KKR with 13 sixes and 10 fours. This innings made us believe that IPL was the right advertising platform.

Havells was sold on IPL from then on. We spent large sums of money and got high viewership.

Only in 2010, when IPL was estimated to be worth over $4 billion as a league and the viewership remained huge did we tinker with our advertising tactics. We felt that ad rates had zoomed too much and, to save costs, we wanted to invest tactfully in IPL. We decided to advertise more aggressively at certain moments of the match, like towards the end of the first innings, and the final few overs of the game.

We thought that the viewership was the highest at these stages of the matches and, hence, we would benefit more from such advertising. The plan did not work out, and we shifted back to our original blueprint in the 2011 season.

The IPL and cricket, in many ways, transformed the image of the Havells brand and of the group. We became the top-of-mind brand for electrical goods among the consumers. Given the popularity of the league, and in spite of the allegations of betting and match fixing, we leveraged huge advantages.

To give an example, the advertising rate for a ten-second slot for the finals of the first IPL season between Rajasthan Royals and Chennai Super Kings, owned by then BCCI chairman N. Srinivasan's India Cements, was Rs 10 lakh, or higher than the rate for the T20 finals between India and Pakistan in 2007!

The TRP for the above game was 9.8 per cent among cable and satellite TV households, or the highest for any cricket match played in India. At the franchise level, the viewership among home audiences, or the states where the cities were located, was, on average, 14 per cent (of cable and satellite households) for Mumbai Indians, 13 for Chennai Super Kings and 11.6 for Kolkata Knight Riders.

Entertainment programmes on TV, like the generally popular serials suffered a huge dip in viewership during the key IPL games. According to an article in the *Economic Times*, Star Plus's *Kya Aap Panchvi Pass Se Tez Hain* was the most impacted by the IPL semi-finals on 30 and 31 May. Despite Shah Rukh Khan's presence, *Panchvi Pass* posted its lowest rating of 1.32 and 1.74 since the show began.

We were wedded to cricket after IPL for our branding and communication. We were there during the West Indies tour of India, the Sri Lanka tour of India and the 2009 Champion's League, a new format that emerged out of IPL-like formats in India and other cricket-playing nations.

We discontinued our association with the Champion's League, but cricket became our horse to ride to victory in the marketplace.

Apart from heavy advertising, we took more measured steps to give ourselves a well-rounded corporate identity.

TWENTY

Fans Forever

Sometime in 2008, Paul Griswold, then CEO of Sylvania, brought a problem to our attention. We had renamed the company Havell's Sylvania after acquiring it. That's because we were called Havell's. Such a name, he said, implied Sylvania of Havells and, in some way, turned Sylvania into a lesser brand.

QRG was very careful about such things. Even when it had come to naming his first venture, a lot of people had suggested the name Guptajee Electricals. After all, he was getting into the electrical business and this would create the right associations in the mind of the buyer. Instead, he chose to call it Guptajee & Co. in order to keep it open-ended—what if he got into some other business later, such as automobile components?

He saw logic in Griswold's argument and ordered that we drop the apostrophe as early as possible. That's how our company came to be called Havells.

Actually, as Narayanan found out when he joined the group in 2005, the name of Havells was spelt differently in different communications, brochures and product literature. It was generally either Havell's, Havell or Havells. This was bad for our corporate image. A keen observer may have found us callous.

'It was years later that we standardized the name to Havells. When I joined, the most commonly used spelling in internal communications was Havell's, which indicated that there were several companies and brands under the umbrella group of Havell. The media too used different spellings, and sometimes in the same article,' Narayanan would recall.

The same was true about Havells's logo, albeit in another manner. In a country where its demographics had undergone dramatic changes, with majority of Indians below thirty years of age, the logo was conservative and outdated. There was an urgent need to present Havells as the brand for the young generation, which was more educated, street-smart, savvy, confident, ambitious and better off.

There was another issue. Our logo was a red triangle. And others in the switchgear business like Standard Electricals and Larsen & Toubro too had taken on a similar logo. By default, it had become the industry logo. If we had to stand out from the clutter, we needed to take on a new one.

When Narayanan talked about the changes in logo and brand name, I agreed immediately. QRG raised a few questions about the timing but grasped the significance quickly. He realized that 2008 was the right time to effect these changes to catapult the Havells brand name on to another level. The brief to the design firm, Locus Design of Pune, was crystal clear.

The final logo design was exactly what we had wished for. It reflected the identity of the new Havells brand, and also the group, in the twenty-first century. In place of the red triangle, we now had 'the global H'.

The H was meant to signify a strong connection with Havells. The red colour denoted continuity from the past. The ample curves on the H were indicative of a dynamic, contemporary and global brand. Most importantly, 'the global H' had a 3-D effect, which was representative of our leadership, the ever-expanding breadth of our products and services, and our global presence.

'I realized months after the new logo was introduced that there seemed to be an external force which drove the future destiny of Havells. Coincidentally, the new logo looked uncannily similar to the aerial overview of our new headquarters at Noida, which was constructed around the same time as the birth of the logo.

'For the 175–seat auditorium on the fifth floor of the office, we had ordered furniture from China. It too looked like the new logo. The external covers of the power-cord holders used at the Noida office seemed similar to the new logo,' Narayanan would remember.

All this time, our ads were being appreciated all around. That's because while others made films for as little as Rs 1 lakh, ours cost anywhere between Rs 30 lakh and Rs 60 lakh. Like in every other matter, we would go with only the best. This consciousness was now a part of our DNA.

While most of the ads worked well, there were a few that didn't. One, for our fans, showed people in an office wading in a pool of sweat. The feedback we got was that people found it repulsive; nobody wanted to even think about a sweat pool. Another one, this time for our CFL lamps, showed an executioner who, after a hard day's work, does his bit for energy conservation by switching on a Havells lamp. That too didn't click and we withdrew it immediately. But such instances weren't many.

Even when Balki first met us, we were very clear that we did not want a brand ambassador. We wanted our products to be the hero. We didn't want to share the limelight with others. Often, when they see a celebrity, people fail to connect with the product. We didn't want this to happen to us. Balki shared this view—this way, he would be able to explore his creativity better.

Then Balki came up with a suggestion that would give a huge fillip to our brand image. He proposed a campaign around the theme of fans—supporters. What and how? We had no idea. But the concept appealed to us.

Initially, we thought of roping in Kapil Dev but realized that he was not as popular as Sachin Tendulkar, and the campaign would not make an impact. Then another name came up for discussion—Rajesh Khanna.

Rajesh Khanna was the original superstar of Bollywood. In the late sixties and early seventies, he gave a string of unprecedented hits. Such was his popularity that women used to send him letters written in blood. There used to be a throng of visitors at his house every day hoping to catch a glimpse of him. Producers queued up in front of his house with large signing bonuses. Whatever he touched turned into gold.

And he truly lived life king size. According to one account, the bungalow he lived in was bought from actor

Rajinder Kumar. Various estimates put its current value at upwards of Rs 200 crore. He named it Ashirwad, or blessing, so that all fan mail that came to him would say Rajesh Khanna Ashirwad, or bless Rajesh Khanna, on the envelope. Such was his success that he even gifted a bungalow to his then girlfriend, Anju Mahendru. According to a recent book on the superstar, she still lives in that house.

His success, and his ways, form an integral part of Bollywood folklore.

Rajesh Khanna made it big, even though there was no sophisticated public relations machinery to work on his image and enhance his popularity—no social media to mould public opinion. All the adulation he got, especially from women of all ages, was genuine. It shows that in his time, stars had to manage the media on their own, without advisers and specialists. And Khanna played the game really well. He handed out scoops to friendly journalists whenever he had to settle personal scores and upstage rivals. One journalist who was close to him and who made much capital of that closeness was Devyani Chaubal. So much so, the headgear at his wedding was tied by none other than Chaubal, says a new book, called *Rajesh Khanna*, written by Yasser Usman.

His fall was no less dramatic. After a brief, though stellar, reign at the top, Rajesh Khanna was unseated by Amitabh Bachchan, who played the role of the 'angry young man' to perfection. That was the time when unemployment among educated youngsters had started to soar, leading to frustration all around. State-led growth had run out of steam. There were lockouts and unrest. Discontent was writ large all over the country. The angry young man's persona captured the mood of the nation quite well.

As a result, Rajesh Khanna's carefully crafted lover-boy image got dumped by the wayside almost overnight. There were few takers for his films. The producers who made a beeline to his home in the past now began to avoid him. According to Usman's book, the superstar manipulated his wedding with Dimple Kapadia, who was all of sixteen then, to resurrect his lover boy image, which had taken a beating after a series of flops. But that too didn't help. Nothing could arrest the plunge in his fortunes.

This brought out another facet of Rajesh Khanna— he became insecure and possessive, and perhaps a little vindictive too. According to the book, when he was getting married to Dimple Kapadia, he insisted the raucous wedding procession take a detour and pass in front of Mahendru's house! His marriage with Kapadia ended in separation, not divorce, again because of the possessive streak in Khanna.

Usman traces the reasons for this obsessive behaviour to Khanna's childhood—his parents, residents of Amritsar, had given him away to his childless uncle and aunt who brought him up in Bombay. Khanna always kept his original family under wraps, though his private staff would recount his grief at his sister's death. They would also recall the secret visits of Khanna's brother who bore an uncanny resemblance to the superstar.

In spite of such traits, Rajesh Khanna remained a superstar. According to one commentator, what made Rajesh Khanna special among all Bollywood personalities was that he was a bundle of contradictions—a megalomaniac and a loner, capricious and magnanimous, pompous and insecure, possessive and vindictive, successful and a failure. His flops had not taken away his aura—and the fact remains that nobody had even come close to the kind of adulation he received.

In early 2011, Rajesh Khanna was diagnosed with cancer after it had reached an advanced stage.

Balki's idea was to associate Rajesh Khanna's legendary fan following with our fans.

We were a little sceptical. He was, after all, a spent force. His prime had passed almost forty years ago. Agreed he was a superstar like no other in his time, but that was in the previous generation. The current generation had no connection whatsoever with him. We also knew that, because of the cancer, he had lost a lot of weight and was now a frail copy of his old self. The sight of a sick man is not a pleasant one.

To cut a long story short, we were unsure how the audience would react to Rajesh Khanna.

But Balki was very positive right from the beginning. His storyline was quite simple—Rajesh Khanna would be in the company of Havells fans and then say, in his trademark manner, 'Nobody can steal my fans from me.'

By now, we had come to trust Balki fully. He too would tell people that Havells was his favourite account. We had faith in his instincts. After much internal debate, we gave him the go-ahead. Balki offered to add more punch to it by including Bachchan in the ad. Since he had walked away with Rajesh Khanna's fans, it was proposed that Bachchan would enter the film late and bow to Rajesh Khanna.

We liked the idea. Balki had an excellent relationship with Bachchan, and had directed him in two films—*Cheeni Kum* and *Paa*. He took this proposal to Bachchan but he refused—he said he didn't want to take the limelight away from Rajesh Khanna. This was old-world courtesy at its best.

So, we decided to go ahead with Rajesh Khanna alone. Sikka got in touch with him early in 2012. Through some acquaintances, he established contact with Rajesh Khanna. To break the ice, Sikka spoke to him in Punjabi. In spite of his fragile health, Sikka got the sense that the ex-superstar was keen to do the film.

Rajesh Khanna, actually, had not done a single advertisement or endorsement in his life! His was a simple era—Rajesh Khanna's only source of income was his films. Today, the business model of stars is different—films keep them in the public consciousness, while the real money they collect comes from endorsements and stage shows. Many have transited smoothly into business.

As this was to be a whole new experience, Rajesh Khanna was a little apprehensive. But Sikka made him feel comfortable. Khanna laid down three conditions—one, the agreement would be just one page long; two, there would be no negotiations over the fees; and three, we would have to pay all the money upfront.

We had thought he would charge Rs 5–10 lakh for the assignment, and were therefore a bit surprised when he asked for Rs 50 lakh. We agreed. A lot of people felt it was a case of throwing good money after bad, but we had full faith in Balki's ability to deliver. Rajesh Khanna also told Sikka, in Punjabi, 'This will be an ad you will never forget.'

It was common knowledge that Rajesh Khanna had fallen on hard times and needed the money badly. With the money we paid him, he bought a luxury car for his younger daughter, Rinke, according to one rumour.

The IPL season was slated to start from 13 April. We wanted to be ready with the ad by then. But then our phone calls to him started going unanswered. We were worried— was Rajesh Khanna once again up to his infamous tantrums? Then we were told by his personal staff that he had fallen down in the bathroom and suffered a hairline fracture in his leg.

Usman's book carries interesting details of the shoot. According to it, Rajesh Khanna's condition worsened after he had confirmed the dates for the shoot. Thanks to the fracture in his leg, there was so much pain and swelling that he couldn't even wear his shoes.

This is the time we got in touch with Dimple Kapadia, Rajesh Khanna's estranged wife and she promised to help us. The new date for the shoot was 18 April. While his aides doubted if he would be able to do the shoot, Rajesh Khanna asked to be taken to the Nanavati Hospital for treatment. After two days, he drove from the hospital straight to the airport and took the flight to Bangalore with Dimple Kapadia, where the shoot was supposed to take place inside a stadium.

That same night, Balki explained the shot to Rajesh Khanna after dinner. It was decided that Khanna would walk into the frame with the famous song, *Ye shaam mastani*, from his film *Kati Patang*, playing in the background like an anthem. Before going home, Rajesh Khanna showed Balki his walk that had made a million hearts skip a beat more than forty years ago.

The next day, Rajesh Khanna came for the shoot and quickly changed into a tuxedo with a white shirt and bow tie. As his vanity car was parked some distance away from the stadium where the shoot was to take place, he covered the distance in a wheelchair—he had become so frail.

But from the moment Balki said 'lights, camera, action' till he said 'pack up' late in the evening, Rajesh Khanna was professionalism personified. He was perhaps transported back to his glory days, when every shot he gave was lapped up by his fans.

Before the 2012 season of the IPL, we launched this almost-extraordinary TV advertisement that came with the tag line, 'Havells, fans are forever'. In our minds, the ad presented a perfect combination of celebrity, nostalgia and brand-connect. It showed Rajesh Khanna reminiscing about his glorious past and his loyal followers. It ended with a twist—he still had the fans, except they were the quality products manufactured by Havells.

For us, the ad achieved several objectives. One, it enabled the company to create visibility in the fans market, which is not a much-talked-about category and where campaigns by most competitors in India are similar.

In an interview, Prasoon Joshi, executive chairman and CEO, McCann Worldgroup, admitted as much when he said, 'Sometimes ads are made not to hardsell a product but to start a conversation or create a language for the brand,' which is what the Rajesh Khanna ad did.

Two, it allowed us to break out of the communication clutter, which is our endeavour in any brand promotion exercise. Most brand experts contend that to break through the marketplace clutter, 'brand promotion must engage customers at key passion points'.

The choice of Rajesh Khanna fit this bill. 'When the ad was being conceived we could think of none other than Rajesh Khanna himself who had the maximum fan following, almost legendary, and who still commands a great deal of respect,' Balki would recollect.

On his part, Rajesh Khanna maintained a stoic, almost respectful, distance. 'To be approached after so many years is indeed a great honour for me and I am delighted to connect with my fans once again. Shooting after a gap of so many years has definitely brought back fond memories and I feel that not a lot has changed at all.'

Obviously, there were a few critics who felt that ad was in a bad taste. They thought the ad was like a 'living obituary' for Rajesh Khanna and it aroused the feelings of whether to cry for the aged superstar or console him for the loss of his real fan following.

However, at Havells we thought that the ad served its purpose. It created a strong relationship between the brand, product and celebrity. Fans as a product became a good communication substitute for fans of a former Bollywood actor.

A few months later, on 18 July 2012, to be precise, Rajesh Khanna died. His last words were 'pack up'. After that, we took the campaign off air.

I am often asked if we see a spike in sales after every successful campaign. The honest answer is 'no'. That's because the kind of products we make are not impulse purchases—one buys fans, CFL lamps, LEDs, switches, geysers, wires and appliances once in a while. The idea is that we should have top-of-mind recall, so that when the buyer goes to the market, he should ask for Havells.

Products like ours go through three stages of brand recall. In the first, the buyer goes and asks the dealer for a fan, and the dealer says, 'Take Havells.' In the second phase, the buyer comes and asks what fans do you have? And when the dealer lists all the brands, the buyer says, 'Give me Havells.' In the third and final stage, the buyer comes and asks for Havells straight away. We are now in the third stage. In more than 50 per cent of the cases, the buyer comes and asks for our products by name.

There were other gains too that flowed in from our advertising campaigns. In most of the categories, we are the clear price leaders. A study to understand Havells brand equity vis-à-vis rivals, carried out by the marketing communication company Millward Brown in December 2014, showed the brand persona as an independent, confident and successful young boy who is about to take over established players. Respondents to the survey found Havells as someone in the late twenties or early thirties, a trendy person, who is fun to hang around with, and yet is competitive and aggressive.

Most of the respondents found us to be more youthful and trendy than others in the market. People also found us to be a holistic, modern and premium brand. They also took note of our strong design and aesthetic sense.

It is not easy managing the Havells brand because it talks to multiple audiences within the family. The brand operates in the age bracket of twenty-six and above. Some of the categories that we operate in, like cables and wires, MCBs, RCCBs and distribution boards, have men as the core target audience who play the role of the influencer, decision maker and buyer. The other categories, such as fans, water heaters, switches and home appliances have the woman of the household as the key influencer and decision maker, though the man is the buyer.

Over time, our advertising budgets have gone up further. We ended 2014–15 with an expenditure of Rs 160 crore. And for 2015–16, we increased the budget to Rs 200 crore—the highest by far in the categories that we operate in. Many multinational corporations were forced to take note of our brand-building exercise. What flummoxed them was how we had transited commodities like MCBs and wires into brands.

Luckily, our advertising juggernaut coincided with the second take-off phase of the Indian economy. The first one happened in the nineties, when the country embarked on the path of economic reforms. Manmohan Singh's new industrial policy in the early nineties hacked the bureaucratic red tape to pieces, economic growth rates were over 6 per cent, 7 per cent and 8 per cent, respectively, in the three financial years (April–March) between 1994 and 1997.

Similarly, during the eight years between 2003 and 2011, India's annual growth was over 8 per cent in six of them; the economy grew over 9 per cent in three of them. Before the growth rate skidded to 6.4 per cent in 2011–12 and 5 per cent in 2012–13, Indian policymakers had taken 8 per cent as the benchmark, and most took it for granted.

The Indian consumers enjoyed the economic ride, and felt that the party would continue forever. They spent confidently, and they leveraged their wealth through easy and cheap credit to acquire assets of all forms. As demand for residential housing and commercial space shot up, it resulted in a boom in real estate and construction sectors. Havells benefited as it translated into higher demand for our products.

More importantly, the new consumer, who was young and smart, richer and acquisitive, took more interest in the interiors of her home and office. Decisions about the purchase of consumer electrical products were no longer dependent on the contractors; architects, designers and buyers came together to decide which brands and what designs to buy. Therefore, advertising in mass media was critical to woo the consumer. We were there with our campaigns at the right time.

We selected the best media buying agency and our advertising agency was one of the best. We shifted our approach from customer management system, or CMS, to Marcom, or marketing and communications. We hired people for the Marcom team, whose strength shot up from nine to forty people in no time. Our in-house team functioned like a mid-size advertising agency. For example, we internally managed the various audio-visual shoots and the design of the products catalogues. We hired employees who had expertise in animation.

The idea behind the in-house team, along with an external advertising agency, was to achieve quick turnaround targets. It helped us to do things faster. For us, speed was of the essence. We did not want to lose a day. We knew that we would make mistakes. But the idea was not to repeat them and use the learning to do better next time.

The headquarters supported the branches, which were the soul of our success. The Marcom team armed the branches with everything related to marketing and branding, and provided state-level managers with ground support.

Because of these efforts, and economic growth, trade circles got more and more excited about Havells's products. Our distributors and dealers found it easier to sell our products as the consumers were aware of them due to the mass advertising initiatives. Everything was rationalized within the distribution system—from trade discounts to credit periods.

A further fillip was provided to our dealers because of our concept of Galaxy Stores. We wanted our existing and potential customers, including professionals like architects and interior designers, to experience the entire range of our products in a single place. But since distributors and dealers have different priorities, and most of them cannot showcase all our products, we felt we could do it through our own chain of stores.

Today, the number of Galaxy Stores across the country has crossed the 250 mark; the annual turnover of these stores is in excess of Rs 700 crore. Moreover, our buyer knows the range we have to offer, and how Havells can solve all her needs for household electricals and appliances.

Today, Havells's brand equity is its biggest asset. We have managed to do what few Indian business houses can claim to do—faced with competition from multinational corporations, unlike us, many have simply thrown in the towel.

TWENTY-ONE

Deal-making from the ICU

The Sylvania experience changed QRG. Though we had brought it back on track, he knew we had come close to disaster—by taking our eyes off the company. He now wanted to ensure that such an incident did not happen again. The turnaround of Sylvania was indeed a matter of honour for him but it had also exposed our vulnerable side. He felt he needed to be better informed about the affairs of his business at all times. We couldn't afford another slip-up.

QRG's need to be firmly in control at all times began to assert itself. He became sterner, impatient, and a kind of control freak. He became paranoid about preserving the culture and legacy of Havells. This was because he knew that lack of cultural integration with Sylvania was a mistake.

At the same time, QRG's health had begun to deteriorate. In 2008, he went through a bypass surgery. His kidneys too were damaged. After much delay, he was put on dialysis from 2011.

These two factors made him a man in a hurry. At times, I felt he was in a great rush to pass on all the wisdom he had acquired over the years to me and to the rest of the team at Havells. From being a patient listener, he became more of a speaker and teacher.

This unsettled many people in the organization, especially those who didn't know him well. Some would even complain to me about this. QRG's new avatar called for patience from my side, but it was okay. I did not want to send out any signal that father and son were not on the same page. I did not want to get into a situation where there were two power centres within Havells.

QRG, of course, was in no mood to slow down. Nine out of ten sons would have wanted their father, if his physical condition was like QRG's, to take it easy, even retire. But I knew the frustration he would suffer at home would be far greater than the discomfort he felt in office. Work was his medicine. His wife would often ask him to take rest but he just wasn't built that way.

By now, he would listen to just one or two people; I was one of them. On days that my mother felt he was in no position to work, she used to ask me to ground him. But even if his health was 60 per cent okay, I would not object to his going to work. Once at work, he would be his old self, bubbling with enthusiasm and ideas, taking quick decisions, etc.

I knew of other business leaders who had similar enthusiasm for work even in their old age. Captain C.P. Krishnan Nair, who founded the Leela chain of hotels and was active even in his nineties (born in February 1922, he died in May 2014), and Brijmohan Lall Munjal, the chairman of Hero MotoCorp (he finally relinquished control to his son, Pawan Kant, in June 2015, and became the chairman emeritus of his company) was also working in his early nineties. If they could work well past conventional retirement age, so could QRG. I fully empathized with his need to be in the office.

Sometime in 2010, we felt that we must get into newer areas in order to grow. But we didn't know what. The only thing we were clear about was that we should be able to leverage our existing distribution network to sell these products. After much deliberation, we shortlisted four items—air conditioners, geysers, kitchen appliances and water-lifting pumps. We formed four teams—one for each product category—to study the prospects and suggest an entry strategy.

The most ambitious of these projects was air conditioners. The market was booming. That was the first attraction. Second, we had spoken to several of our dealers. Though traditionally air conditioners have never been sold through electrical stores, they were fairly confident that they could do so. We also felt we could develop the channel to sell air conditioners, and later get into the other channels—multi–product consumer electronics stores and stand-alone air conditioner stores.

The team, which included people who had worked with Voltas and other top companies, had also identified some suppliers in China. The idea was to import the machines initially, and once we achieved scale, we would manufacture them in the country. And we wanted to play in the premium space—as always.

QRG had always taken great inspiration from Reliance Industries' Vimal brand of fabric. It was premium but was still backed by very large production capacities and a nationwide distribution network. So, it became a premium product for the mass market. That is where he wanted Havells to play in all product categories. For air conditioners, we wanted to be in the same category as Daikin.

In spite of all the progress we made, we finally decided to call off the air conditioner venture.

There were a few reasons for it. To begin with, in all our previous brand extensions, 25 to 30 per cent of the business had come from the existing dealer network. Here, it would be zero. We were not convinced that our dealers would be able to sell air conditioners as well. Two, the business had become extremely competitive. Most of our businesses gave us a profit margin of at least 10 per cent; in air conditioners, the industry leaders, LG and Samsung, were working at 5 to 6 per cent margins, in spite of the large turnover.

And three, while Indian brands like Voltas were doing quite well, we felt that to enter a market where so many brands had fallen by the wayside would be a big risk. LG and Samsung were global players and had a strong pipeline of products. Also, they had started to manufacture in India, which had brought down their costs. Our strategy to import from China would not work.

We had no such reservations about geysers and home appliances. We decided to launch geysers first and then follow up with appliances.

Geysers were a Rs 2000-crore per annum market, though a seasonal one—people bought them only in winter. The geysers we brought to the market in 2012 were enamel coated and had a plastic body, which offered better insulation. There was nothing like our geysers in the market. Our price was 40–50 per cent above rivals like Racold and Bajaj, but the product was well received.

After us, new players like A.O. Smith and Haier also entered the premium end of the market. We closed 2014–15 with a turnover of Rs 100 crore in this product category. Then, in early 2015, our own geyser factory at Neemrana became functional. Put up at a cost of Rs 100 crore, it is the most modern geyser plant in India. And it counts among the most automated ones in the world—just forty people there make 300,000 geysers in a year.

Appliances made up a bigger category at Rs 5000 crore per annum. But it needed careful planning. We wanted to be in the premium segment—on par with Philips and Morphy Richards, if not better. We also had to have the right products. Though mixer-grinders and household irons make up around 60–70 per cent of the appliances market, we decided to have a full line across garment care, food processing and brewing.

The bane of the appliances industry is the large presence of the unorganized sector. It thrives on evasion of taxes and uses inferior material, and therefore its price tags are very low. In a highly price sensitive market like India, this becomes important. Also, the market is fragmented. Apart from the national brands, there are strong regional ones. For instance, Butterfly and Preethi (now owned by Philips) are strong in the south.

In spite of these deterrents, we decided to take the plunge. We knew that appliances were sold through the electrical counter as well as the kitchen counter. We felt that while we could readily enter the first, the second we could do subsequently.

In the past, there used to be a powerful brand called Sumeet. According to one account, Sumeet came into being after Satya Prakash Mathur's wife asked him to fix her Braun mixer that had broken down. An engineer with Siemens, Mathur designed a mixer with a powerful motor that could stand the rigours of Indian grinding. It was a killer machine. In 1963, he floated a company called Power Company Appliances to make mixers on a commercial scale.

Sumeet became a runaway success—it was a must in all south Indian trousseaus.

Unfortunately, because of some family issues, the business went into decline and, at one stage, we learnt that it was on the block. We received some feelers for it, but we decided to press ahead with our own brand. We designed the products in-house and contracted vendors in China and India to make them for us, till we achieved critical mass.

The arrangement worked well. We launched our appliances in 2013, supported by a strong television campaign. In 2014–15, we did almost Rs 170-crore business in this category.

Then in 2014, we entered water-lifting pumps. We manufactured them at Neemrana. Pumps are also sold through the electrical channel. There is a separate pump channel too, which we plan to tap later.

In April 2014, we came to know of another acquisition possibility that sent our pulse racing one more time.

The history of Crompton Greaves can be traced back to Colonel R.E.B. Crompton who, in 1878, founded an enterprise called R.E.B. Crompton & Co. in England to manufacture electrical equipment. This company merged with F.&.A. Parkinson, which led to the formation of Crompton Parkinson. In 1937, this company established its wholly owned Indian subsidiary, Crompton Parkinson Works, in Bombay, along with a sales organization called Greaves & Crompton Parkinson. In 1947, the company was taken over by Lala Karamchand Thapar. In 1966, he merged the two companies to form Crompton Greaves.

In the Thapar family settlement that took place in the early noughties, Crompton Greaves came into the possession of Gautam Thapar. It had three lines of business—power systems, industrial systems and consumer products.

The dashing Thapar, whose parents had at one time contemplated a career in films for him, expanded Crompton Greaves' footprint abroad quickly. In 2005, he acquired the Belgium-based Pauwels Group, which gave Crompton Greaves manufacturing facilities in Belgium, Ireland, the USA, Canada and Indonesia, and followed it with a series of other acquisitions—Ganz in Hungary in 2006, Microsol in Ireland in 2007, Sonomatra in France and MSE in the USA in 2008, as well as PTS in the UK in 2010.

The global slowdown that began in 2008 affected the industrial and power systems businesses of Crompton Greaves. Soon, the company was heavily in debt. Finally, Thapar put the consumer products business up for sale—fans, lights, appliances and pumps.

Once we got to know of this opportunity, we engaged Standard Chartered as our investment banker. Internally, we came to the conclusion that we would be able to pay up to Rs 5000 crore for it—in cash and stock. It would stretch us, of course, but, as we discussed it internally, it began to look doable.

QRG was greatly excited about the deal. Even in his final days, when he was in the ICU, he would remove his oxygen mask and inquire about its progress.

The talks progressed well. Finally, Thapar asked me to come to London for talks. I booked the tickets. I had met Thapar in 2004 when we had all gone on a trip to China organized by Standard Chartered. He was warm and charming, and spoke freely of the earlier mismanagement of his companies. In the corporate world, he had won accolades for turning around Ballarpur Industries, the country's largest paper company, as well as Crompton Greaves.

Just before I was to leave for London, we met one of his key executives at the Oberoi in Delhi. He told us that they were looking at other options too; in fact, he said, they weren't even sure if they wanted to sell the business. Somehow, we began to feel that they had had a change of heart.

Soon, I got a call from Thapar that I need not come to London and that we would meet when he was in Delhi next. This confirmed our suspicion. When we met, he reiterated that he was looking at various options.

Then, in April 2015, it was announced that private equity funds Advent International and Temasek had agreed to buy 35 per cent in Crompton Greaves' consumer products division for Rs 2000 crore. The value they offered to Thapar was higher than what we had in mind.

On 7 November 2014, QRG passed away. He finally lost the battle to his various ailments. But he was at peace. One of the last people to talk to him was Vickyji. The evening before QRG died, Vickyji had gone to meet him in the ICU. QRG told him that he had done all his karma. He had a smile on his face and had placed his hands on the pillows. Vickyji would later recount that QRG looked like a king on his throne. He was perfectly in control of his senses, sipping tea, munching on a sandwich and talking about business.

The next morning, he was no more.

Blessed are those who go like this. We didn't shut down our factories and offices; that's not how he would have wanted it. The show had to go on. It was left to me to carry his legacy forward.

TWENTY-TWO

Epilogue: The Legend Lives On . . .

Some years ago, my son Abhinav, who was greatly inspired by QRG, said at the dining table one evening that he was Qimat Rai Gupta II. I told him for that he would have to change his name to Abhinav Rai Gupta. The matter was forgotten after that. But I felt my name, Anil Gupta, was sort of lightweight. I had earlier shared with QRG that I wanted a weighty name like his—one which people remember once they hear it. So, in January 2013, both my son and I changed our names: he became Abhinav Rai Gupta and I took the name Anil Rai Gupta. Aradhana, my daughter, also changed her name to Aradhana Rai Gupta subsequently. This is how a bit of QRG has come into our names.

That both my kids were doing well in studies was a matter of immense satisfaction for QRG. When Aradhana got admission into an undergraduate course in economics (honours) in the prestigious St. Stephen's College, he was simply overjoyed. Ours was a happy household. Apart from his grandchildren, QRG was very close to Sangeeta, my wife. He was extremely fond of his daughter-in-law.

I was an unabashed lifelong fan of QRG. As I worked closely with him for twenty years, I learnt the way he built businesses and motivated people. I had big shoes to fill, but I had to try.

QRG's opinion of me was mixed. There were times when he would praise me in front of hundreds of people and say that I was ready to take the baton from him; then, on another day, he would tell me that I still had a lot to learn.

These contradictions did not bother me too much. I understood that any self-made man would have such apprehensions about his son.

A first-generation entrepreneur, like QRG, is a rare person—daring, bold, adventurous and somewhat rash. It was in his character to take risks. He is a pioneer of sorts. They are different from ordinary folks. His courage of conviction defies logic, and his trust of his instinct can scare the wits out of rational people.

For example, many Americans feel they have superior genes because their forefathers were pioneers—they gave up everything they had in Europe to start life afresh in a new, and largely uninhabited, place. This was a risk of the most extraordinary proportions, yet they took it.

History is what great people make it, and greatness comes to those who are ready to risk it all. It is difficult for others to understand the psyche of a pioneer, a first-generation entrepreneur, the incorrigible risk-taker.

Success doesn't come easy. This makes the pioneers really strong from within. Their resilience runs deep. A few knocks here and there mean nothing to them.

The second generation, perhaps because it gets everything on a platter, does not have the same aggression and mental toughness. There is a certain softness about them. Their mental make-up is different from the previous generation—it need not be inferior, they are just on different wavelengths.

I have often seen that the father eats, sleeps and breathes the business, but it fails to ignite the same passion in the son.

This worries the father. He begins to wonder what will happen to the business once he retires. The niggling doubt about the son's ability makes him reluctant to give up the reins. Many, therefore, assign their sons small or peripheral jobs, like the responsibility for a factory, and run their company themselves even after they have sailed past retirement age. This is a recipe for disaster— it narrows the son's vision, which deprives him of the wider perspective and plays havoc with his confidence.

Unfortunately, the sons are often unable to make sense of this divergence in world view. The result is discontent and strife. Some choose to rebel against their parents, displaying what in business parlance is called the Aurangzeb Syndrome, while some choose to suffer in silence. Many struggle all their lives to gain the respect of their father. The end result is the same—father exasperated with his son, and son unable to figure out how to work with his father.

I have been a keen student of history, and this tectonic shift within a generation did not escape my notice. In several families that I know, this is a serious issue. A situation like this can be diffused the moment the son realizes where the father is coming from. All it requires is some patience and understanding.

In our case, whenever QRG said something, I tried to put it into the right context—why did he say what he said? Once I analysed it in this fashion, all doubts simply vanished.

For example, QRG would at times say that I do not have his aggression and wanted me to be as assertive as he was (a lot of business historians say the killer instinct reduces in the second generation and gets totally wiped out in the third generation; maybe it's true), but I think I know fairly well what he had in mind for Havells. He wanted it to be honest, transparent, nimble and quick. I understood his business philosophy—focus on distribution, stay close to the dealer and play in the top end of the market. Everything else flows from that.

I knew that all I had to do was walk down the same road. Thus, in the first five months of 2015, I visited each and every branch of Havells and met as many as 2000 dealers.

Am I an exact replica of QRG? I can't be that. I don't have to be that. But as long as my objectives are the same as his, it doesn't matter. Of course, I am different from him in more ways than one. For example, QRG was not very process driven, but I am. At times, he used to comment that I was more bothered about the process than the objective, the journey than the destination, but that's how I am, and he learnt to live with it. However, I have tried to ensure that adherence to procedures should not lead to bureaucracy—that can be fatal for an organization.

But on the goals there was never any disagreement. Whatever QRG wanted Havells to do, I decided to press ahead with it, with more youth and vigour.

Nimbleness and an open mind are of the utmost importance in business—their importance cannot be overemphasized. QRG's lesson is as true in our times as it was in his.

QRG was passionate about Havells. It was on top of his mind all the time. At an emotional level too, he was fully engaged with the business. It would be an understatement to say that the business was dear to him. He had made sacrifices, he had worked through pain for the sake of Havells. But he was also a practical man. He would always say if it was required, we should shut down a business (as indeed we had done in the case of meters) or maybe even sell it. In short, he would not let sentiment or attachment derail his plans. The objective was Havells's growth and selling an asset was for him as reasonable as buying an asset. These were two sides of the same coin.

QRG had, in the last ten or fifteen years, desired to make Havells an institution. He would often tell me that Havells should become like Siemens—nobody remembers the people who founded it over 100 years ago, while everybody knows the products it makes. Havells too he said, should reach such a state in a matter of fifty years.

That sent me on a quest to find out how family businesses can be preserved and carried forward in the long run. In the initial stages, the business is for the family. It provides the family with the means to sustain itself. But once it grows big, the roles get reversed—the family is for the business. It is the family's job to see how the business can grow—it is not there to just provide food and shelter for the family. In this, if the family has to relinquish control, so be it.

In the West, this is a well-accepted practice, but not in India. Few families have had the courage to move out of executive roles and hand over the reins to the professionals. The only instance that comes to mind is the Burman family of Dabur. The company is run fully by professional managers, though the family has some representation on the board. The Burmans also have a family council in which all issues related to their large family are discussed.

Actually, in India, there isn't full agreement on this. Several families, and some experts, feel that the entrepreneurial spirit, which is so vital for growth, can only be provided by a promoter, not by professional managers. Would Reliance Industries have achieved what it has achieved if it wasn't helmed by the Ambani family? These are valid questions.

But we knew what path to take. QRG was never in favour of putting family members in key positions. As far back as in 2000, he used to tell his people—make the directors (family members) redundant. He wanted them to take decisions, and was willing to forgive honest mistakes. He felt offended whenever somebody called him the owner of Havells—he would say, 'I am the chief servant of the company.'

At his death, there were only two family members on the Havells board—Surjitji and me. To fill the vacancy created by QRG's death, Ameet was appointed on the board—that's it. There were suggestions that maybe we should induct my mother and my wife too on the board, but I didn't find it necessary. Instead, I nominated two independent members—Mohandas Pai and Puneet Bhatia, the head of TPG, the private equity fund.

As a result, the Havells board of twelve has only three family members and one executive director, Rajesh Gupta.

I am sure QRG would have approved of it.